The Rhythm of Doctrine

A Liturgical Sketch of Christian Faith and Faithfulness

The Rhythm of Doctrine

A Liturgical Sketch of Christian Faith and Faithfulness

John E. Colwell

British Library Cataloguing in Publication Data
A catalogue record for this book is available from the British Library

Unless otherwise stated all biblical quotations are taken from the
NEW INTERNATIONAL VERSION.
Copyright © 1973, 1978, 1984 by International Bible Society.
First published in Great Britain 1979 by Hodder & Stoughton.
Inclusive language version 1995, 1996.

ISBN 978-1-84227-498-9

Typeset by A.R. Cross
Design by James Kessell for Scratch the Sky Ltd
(www.scratchthesky.com)
Print Management by Adare
Printed in Great Britain by J.H. Haynes & Co., Sparkford

Contents

Preface

This book began in reflection on a conversation. I was sitting in a restaurant with my friend, Prof. John Webster, having just examined a PhD thesis. John and I have known one another for well over twenty years—we were postgraduate students at the same time, researching related themes (but in different places), though our lives since then have followed very different pathways—we were talking about current writing projects and speculating about the possibility of, one day, attempting studies of dogmatics. 'What structure would you follow', asked John, 'if you were ever to write a Systematic Theology?'[1] Since I had never given the matter serious thought (systematic theologies are usually written by notable scholars towards the end of a career—and I do not consider myself 'notable', and I hope I am not yet quite at the end of a career), I responded that I would, of course, comply with the tradition and structure a dogmatics around the articles of the Christian Creed. But reflecting on the matter during my journey home and subsequently, I began to question this standard assumption.

There is nothing wrong, of course, in structuring a systematic theology around the articles of the Creed—beginning with the doctrine of God, then treating the doctrine of Christ, the doctrine of the Spirit, and the doctrine of the Church, and perhaps prefixing the whole with an introductory prolegomena on the doctrine of revelation—this is the structure adopted (albeit rather differently) by John Calvin, Karl Barth, and countless other similarly notable (and rather less notable) writers. But it is not without its flaws: the tendency to treat the doctrine of creation under the heading of the doctrine of God and to treat the doctrine of the atonement under the heading of the doctrine of the Son too easily implies both a division of the Trinity and a separation of creation and redemption that are problematic and unhelpful, the relegation of the Holy Spirit to the third heading furthers this implied division of the Trinity and often tends to focus on the Spirit's rôle in redemption to the detriment of the Spirit's rôle in creation, and a discussion of the Church separate from a discussion of the Trinity runs the risk of focusing on human response rather than on divine mediation. But more fundamentally, although the Christian Creeds find their origin and proper location in the Church's worship, this traditional structuring of dogmatics too readily loses sight of this doxological origin and context: the temptation is to discuss these themes in detachment and abstraction, dividing the theoretical and the philosophical from the practical and the applied, separating dogmatic

---

[1] I did not have a tape-recorder at the time and this is merely my faulty recollection of the conversation.

confession from spirituality and discipleship. I am certainly not implying that those who have adhered to this traditional structure have succumbed to these faults; I am merely observing that the structure itself encourages such.

But there is another way to structure a dogmatics, an approach more explicitly and self-consciously rooted in the Church's worship, an ordering of dogmatics responding to the rhythm of the pattern of liturgy followed by most Christians for most of the years of the Church's history. To structure a systematic theology around the liturgical pattern of the Christian Year seems so obvious to me that I am sure that someone must have adopted this approach previously (though I remain ignorant of such attempts).[2] The idea for ordering a dogmatics in this manner arose, as I have implied, entirely in response to that conversation with John Webster, subsequently honed through several conversations with other theological friends. But chiefly the structure for dogmatics adopted in this book emerges from my own devotional life and practice, conforming to the devotional life and practice of the Church catholic.[3]

Given that I have already acknowledged systematic theologies to be the prerogative of notable scholars towards the conclusion of their careers, and have similarly acknowledged that I certainly do not qualify on the first count and probably do not qualify on the second, this present book is intended as no more than provisional, and that in two senses. In the first place it is provisional in the sense of being an experiment: I do not know whether a dogmatics structured in this manner will work; whether it will prove adequate or persuasive. I have noted some of the pitfalls inherent in structuring a dogmatics in a more traditional manner but, at least at the beginning of this project, I am blissfully oblivious to the pitfalls inherent in this rather different approach (though I am grateful to friends who have alerted me to some predictable dangers). This then is no more than a provisional experiment and, even more than usual, I must listen attentively to my critics (for one's work to be taken seriously is a distinct honour and one is never taken more seriously than when one is constructively criticised). And, consequent to this first form of provisionality, this book

---

[2] The published work that comes closest to this approach is Geoffrey Wainwright's *Doxology: The Praise of God in Worship, Doctrine and Life—A Systematic Theology* (London: Epworth, 1980). I am grateful to Prof. Wainwright for drawing my attention to a passage in Gerhard Sauter's *Gateways to Dogmatics: Reasoning Theologically for the Life of the Church* (Grand Rapids, MI: Eerdmans, 2003), p 185 (cf. pp. 185-87): 'From the arrangement of the church year we derive a specific rhythm defined by the incursion of God into human history and destiny.'

[3] Throughout this book, as elsewhere, I use the term 'catholic' (not capitalised) to refer to the Christian Church in its essential connectedness and continuity across the world and across the centuries. I use the term 'Catholic' (capitalised) with reference to the Roman Catholic Church.

is provisional also in the sense of being intended as no more than a preliminary sketch, an outline (and no more than an outline) of the manner in which a more thorough and comprehensive account of dogmatics might be developed according to this liturgical structure.[4] Should this experiment be deemed (by me and by others) to be effective it may be followed (eventually) by a series of more detailed and sustained studies, but there is no attempt at such detail in this present and brief outline. Comprehensiveness in any academic discipline is, of course, unattainable: so much has been contributed by so many and even in an extended study, or series of studies, it is impossible to refer to all, less still to respond adequately to all. I trust, however, that even in this brief outline a continual and underlying indebtedness to the tradition is evident even though explicit references are kept to the barest minimum. And references will be kept to a minimum: detailed conversations will be alluded to rather than entered; footnotes will be employed for indicative references and supplementary explanation but not for supportive quotations or extended discussions. I suspect that originality in theology is more of a vice than a virtue and all that is included here is consciously shaped by the tradition. Throughout an indebtedness particularly to Thomas Aquinas, John Calvin, and Karl Barth (not to mention a more immediate indebtedness to Colin Gunton, Robert Jenson, and Stanley Hauerwas) should be obvious, and I hope it is sufficiently acknowledged, but there is no space here for extended critical engagement—this is not the purpose of this book.

As is always the case, and as I have already acknowledged, this book is an outcome of a series of conversations and I am inexpressibly indebted to a series of conversation partners, to former teachers, to colleagues, to students (always the most exacting critics), to theological friends, and to family. Theology is the work of the Church and never that of the isolated individual: it is appropriately conversational. As always I am especially grateful to those who have troubled to read this text and to comment upon it (though I am solely accountable for its remaining flaws), to Ian Randall, to Steve Holmes, and to Rosemary Colwell. Similarly, I am grateful to the members of the postgraduate seminar at Spurgeon's College for their general comments on this project. Again I am grateful to Judy Powles, Librarian at Spurgeon's College, who is so much more than a librarian and without whose careful research on my behalf I would write little of any worth. I am grateful to Robin Parry, acquisitions editor for Paternoster, and to Anthony R. Cross for their persistent confidence in

---

[4] For a recent example of a sketch of dogmatics, with the possibility of a longer study to follow, see Kathryn Tanner's excellent *Jesus, Humanity and the Trinity: A Brief Systematic Theology* (Edinburgh: T & T Clark, 2001).

this project. Finally I am grateful again to Carolyn Evans for the preparation of indices and for her careful checking of final proofs.

John E. Colwell
Advent 2006

Acknowledgements

Author and publisher wish to express their gratitude to the following who have granted permission for the use of material covered by copyright:

To Continuum for the use of prayers from *Celebrating Common Prayer: A version of The Daily Office SSF*, The European Province of the Society of Saint Francis (London: Mowbray, 1992), that have been included at the beginning and ending of each chapter of this book.

Extracts from *The Book of Common Prayer*, the rights in which are vested in the Crown, are reproduced by permission of the Crown's Patentee, Cambridge University Press.

Extracts from *The Alternative Service Book 1980* are copyright © The Board of Finance of the Church of England, 1980; The Archbishops' Council, 1999 and are reproduced by permission.

To the Venerable David Silk and to Continuum for the use of prayers previously included in *Prayers for Use at the Alternative Services* (London: Mowbray, 1980), included at the ending of chapter one and the beginning of chapter three.

To Continuum for the use of prayers previously included in *The Promise of His Glory* (London: Church House Publishing and Mowbray, 1991) used at the beginning of chapter two and the beginning of chapter seven.

Abbreviations

ANF	*Ante-Nicene Father of the Christian Church*, 10 vols, eds. Alexander Roberts and James Donaldson (Edinburgh: T & T Clark/Grand Rapids, MI: Eerdmans, 1993–97 [1885–96]).
ASB	*The Alternative Service Book 1980*, The Church of England (London: Collins, 1980).
BCP	*The Book of Common Prayer*, The Church of England (London: Oxford University Press, n.d.).
CCC	*Catechism of the Catholic Church* (London: Geoffrey Chapman, 1994).
CCP	*Celebrating Common Prayer: A Version of The Daily Office SSF*, The European Province of the Society of Saint Francis (London: Mowbray, 1992).
CD	Karl Barth, *Church Dogmatics*, vols. I–IV, Eng. trans. eds. G.W. Bromiley and T.F. Torrance (Edinburgh: T & T Clark, 1956–75).
IJTS	*International Journal of Systematic Theology.*
Institutes	John Calvin, *Institutes of the Christian Religion*, ed. J.T. McNeill, trans. F.L. Battles (Philadelphia, PA: Westminster Press, 1960).
*NPNF*1	*The Nicene and Post-Nicene Father of the Christian Church,* First Series, 14 vols, ed. Philip Schaff *et al.* (Edinburgh: T & T Clark/Grand Rapids, MI: Eerdmans, 1991–98 [1887–94]).
*NPNF*2	*The Nicene and Post-Nicene Father of the Christian Church,* Second Series, 14 vols, ed. Philip Schaff *et al.* (Edinburgh: T & T Clark/Grand Rapids, MI: Eerdmans, 1994–98 [1887–94]).
PG	*Patrologia graeca*, 162 vols, ed. J.-P. Migne (Paris: Petit-Montrouge, 1857–86).
PL	*Patrologia Latina*, 217 vols, ed. J.-P. Migne (Paris: Petit-Montrouge, 1857–86).
ST	St. Thomas Aquinas, *Summa Theologica*, trans. by Fathers of the English Dominican Province (Westminster, MD: Christian Classics, 1981).
SJT	*Scottish Journal of Theology.*
YE	*The Works of Jonathan Edwards*, gen. ed. (vols 1–2) Perry Miller, gen. ed. (vols 3–9) John E. Smith, gen. ed. (vols 10–23) Harry S. Stout (New Haven, CT: Yale University Press, 1957-).

Introduction

Our Father in heaven,
hallowed be your name,
your kingdom come,
your will be done,
on earth as in heaven.
Give us today our daily bread.
Forgive us our sins
as we forgive those who sin against us.
Lead us not into temptation
but deliver us from evil.
For the kingdom, the power, and the glory
are yours
now and for ever.
Amen.[1]

I owe a great debt to Stanley Hauerwas: I learnt from his example more than from any other source that theology and ethics are a single theme rather than two related themes, and that theology and ethics are learnt and imparted in a context of worship rather than a context of academic detachment. I should have known this already. I should have learnt this from Athanasius, or Calvin, or Barth since each of these (albeit somewhat differently) approached theology in this manner. Most of all I should have learnt this from Thomas Aquinas but again I have Stanley Hauerwas to thank for awakening this prejudiced Protestant to the extraordinary richness of Thomas' thought. I guess I simply grew up with typical mid-twentieth-century Protestant assumptions that Thomas Aquinas was a 'natural' theologian (largely to be ignored) and that doctrine and ethics were, at very best, two related sub-disciplines of theology; that worship happened in chapel and that theology happened in the classroom and the library. I was either too preconditioned or too slow to hear the witnesses to the tradition that were confronting me. I just didn't get it. It was the work of Hauerwas that jolted me out of these vacuous delusions to recognise that which I should have known from the beginning. It was the work of Hauerwas that encouraged me to hear the work of Thomas, but also of Calvin, Barth, and others in a fresh and deeper manner. It was the work of Hauerwas that brought me to change the way I teach, the way I worship, and (I hope) the way I live. I am grateful to so many theological teachers, to Colin Gunton more than any other, but it was reading the work of Stanley Hauerwas that most radically changed my life.

---

[1] *CCP*, back flyleaf.

These changes in my understanding of theology's context and task began a long time ago but, like yeast in dough, this outworking of the kingdom of God has taken a long while to seep through the system. The process isn't complete. This book, perhaps, is part of this on-going process of reorientation. It is one thing, you see, to recognise a truth, but it is another matter to cohere with that truth, to allow that truth to change the manner of your thinking, your teaching, your worship, your living. More than once over the years that I have been teaching in my current post I have completely re-written the courses for which I am responsible: each time trying to integrate doctrine and ethics more thoroughly; each time trying to emphasise the doxological context and shape of all we do. When I read Hauerwas' account of his course on ethics, structured around the eucharistic liturgy,[2] I was challenged yet again to review the manner of my teaching. But even in a seminary context, primarily devoted to preparing men and women for Christian ministry, there is much that militates against such reorientation: students arrive with presuppositions concerning the distinctions between doctrine and ethics; many students arrive with assumptions and prejudices concerning the nature of academic study and the academy itself; some students show (pleasant) surprise when prayer or praise are a part of a lecture or seminar; and I have occasionally despaired of any relation between what occurs in a seminar and what occurs in chapel. And, of course, to teach theology in a university is yet more problematic: Western academia indwells Enlightenment assumptions concerning the possibility (and desirability) of objective detachment—but objective detachment is neither possible nor desirable (in any respect), and theology, properly conceived, cannot conform to these fallacious assumptions without renouncing its integrity. We never truly know anything in detachment; we only ever truly know by indwelling. A knowledge of God other than in the context of worship is no true knowledge of the one who is truly God—or, at least, no Christian thinker in the first thousand years of the Church's history would have recognised it as such. God is only truly known as the one he truly is, as the one who draws our worship; and to know this, the true God, is to love him, to worship him, to serve him:[3]

---

[2] Stanley Hauerwas, 'The Liturgical Shape of the Christian Life: Teaching Christian Ethics as Worship' in *In Good Company: The Church as* Polis (Notre Dame and London: University of Notre Dame Press, 1995), pp. 153-68.

[3] While I have no theological objection to the use of the word 'God' as a pronoun (as in 'Godself', for instance), indeed I sometimes use this construction myself, it is grammatically and stylistically awkward. Though, in the main, I retain the traditional masculine personal pronoun when referring to God this is entirely for stylistic reasons: I trust that I do sufficient in this book and elsewhere to demonstrate that I do not think of God as male and that I am sensitive to the continuing problems of this use of male pronouns.

> Hear O Israel, the Lord our God, the Lord is one. Love the Lord your God with all your heart and with all your soul with all your mind and with all your strength... Love your neighbour as yourself. (Mark 12.29-30)

To know the one who is the true God is not merely a matter of our intellect—though it is certainly that—it is simultaneously a matter of our will, of our affections, of all our powers, of our entire being. And truly to know this, the true God, is to be shaped by that knowledge, to be transformed, to be reoriented in our relationship to other people and to creation itself. There can be no theology, no knowledge of the true God, without worship, and there can be no worship or theology without transformation, without ethics. God is known as the one he is, as the one who confronts us and transforms us in worship and in love. I am certainly not implying that true theology cannot be truly taught in a university context—I have a great many friends who excel in this context—but I am implying that it is difficult; that the context and its underlying assumptions militate against authentic engagement; that integrity and coherence are never easily sustained. The question is not whether theology can or should be taught in a university context. The question is rather how this can be attempted with integrity and coherence; how this can be attempted truthfully.

Most approaches to the teaching of Christian theology, whether volumes of systematics or series of lectures and seminars, adhere more or less closely to a creedal structure, exploring the nature of God, the person and work of Christ, the person and work of the Spirit, the nature and mission of the Church. Indeed, any volume of systematics or course in Christian theology would rightly be deemed inadequate if it did not by some means address these themes. As was acknowledged in the preface of this book there is nothing inherently wrong with this creedal approach and much to commend it: the great creeds of the Christian Church were formulated, at least in part, in response to the Church's confession of its faith in worship, its affirmations and benedictions, and they continue as an integral part of the Church's liturgy, they are recited at Sunday prayer, at baptism, at the Eucharist, and their structure and content are often reflected in the Church's hymnody. But as also was acknowledged in the preface of this book, there are dangers in this approach, especially when these creedal confessions are abstracted from their liturgical context and pressed into the service of systematic theology. All too quickly confession degenerates into mere intellectual assent, worshipful commitment gives way to academic detachment, faithfulness is reduced to dogma. This decline is not inevitable but, once the liturgical context of the creeds is neglected or forgotten, it becomes an ever-present danger. And how great a danger this is in a modernistic climate that habitually disconnects acts from virtues, beliefs from behaviour, decision-making from the continuity of character. Enlightenment and post-Enlightenment culture is marked by disconnectedness, disjunction, and detachment. In such an atmosphere we readily capitulate to mere assent, we abandon worship and commitment for the sake of an entirely fallacious academic distance and rigour.

Moreover, and similarly as acknowledged in the preface to this book, this creedal approach to Christian theology tends towards a dividing of that which, though distinct, should never be separated: a dividing of the persons of the Trinity and a consequent and corresponding dividing of the themes of creation and redemption (not to mention eschatology and ecclesiology) in relation to the distinct persons of the Trinity. No approach to theology or structuring of theological themes can ever be unproblematic: we struggle with inadequate language and limited comprehension to express the inexpressible, to speak of one who is beyond our knowledge, who alone is immortal, invisible, the only God (1 Timothy 1.17); in conversation with one another and with the whole Church in its connectedness across the ages we do the best we can without ever claiming completion or comprehensiveness. As already admitted, there are bound to be flaws in the approach I am presently proposing, of some potential flaws I am aware, of others I am blissfully unaware (and rely on friends and critics to identify), but the approach I am here proposing does, at least, militate against this tendency to divide the persons of the Trinity and to divide (in particular) the doctrines of creation and redemption. By focusing in each of the following chapters on God as 'the one who...' I intend to consider God throughout in both his oneness and his threeness. And as (I will argue) is appropriate to a distinctly 'Christian' theology, I will consider the doctrine of creation and of God's relatedness to the universe specifically in the light of the manner in which God is narrated in the Christian story.

But my primary intent in adopting this rather different approach and structure is to maintain an explicit doxological framework and character for the consideration of each theological theme. I am not a liturgist, but you need no such expertise to recognise that the celebration of the Christian Year is long-standing and ubiquitous. I say 'ubiquitous' but I suspect (anecdotally) that this is less true today than it has been in the relatively recent past and certainly less true than in the pre-Reformation Church. The multiplication of 'independent' churches (as if that which were truly the Church could ever be independent), mostly of baptistic or pentecostalist persuasion, has issued (at least to a degree and in detail) in a neglecting, or even a dismissal, of this traditional rhythm of worship and reflection. Amongst most such churches there is celebration of Christmas, of Easter, and of Pentecost, but there is rarely awareness, less still celebration, of Advent, of Epiphany, of Lent, of Trinity, or of the celebration of the lives of the saints, and there is certainly little awareness of the regular rhythm of 'ordinary' time. I write as a Baptist and some may expect me to conform to this non-conformity of neglect. I write, moreover, as one who teaches in a college founded by a Victorian Baptist preacher who was notorious in his distaste for liturgy. But there has always been a 'high' Baptist tradition, of which contradictorily C.H. Spurgeon was in some respects a part,[4] and though this 'high' tradition is barely represented in the multiplication of independent churches that marked the twentieth century, there has been something of a renaissance of this tradition of Baptist sacramentalism in more recent years (I remain delighted by the number of students from the college in which I teach who embrace spiritual direction, make regular retreats, and are creatively inclusive of a liturgical approach to worship).

A formal and traditional liturgy featured not at all in the home in which I was raised. Prayers were extempore; Scripture was read daily; Christmas and Easter were celebrated; Pentecost (Whitsun) was acknowledged; I recall no mention of Epiphany, or Advent; Lent was a time when Anglicans and Catholics gave up things—but we were neither Anglican nor Catholic, and in the ultra-Protestant context in which I grew up there was little to be given up anyway. When I was about ten years old we began to attend a Baptist church (we had attended a Mission Hall until then) and I was introduced to a very different range of hymns and, in those days, to chants (it was a 'high' Baptist church)—previously I had only known the hymns of Sankey and Moody. Yet even in this very different context there was little sense of the rhythm of the Christian Year, extempore prayer still dominated and responsive readings were rare. And having been ordained as a minister of the gospel within the Baptist Union of Great Britain I perpetuated this tradition (at least until all marks of formality were swept aside by the enthusiasms of the Charismatic Movement). I was (and am) deeply committed to systematic biblical preaching, but there was no adherence to any set lectionary and still little awareness of the Christian Year (though Advent was now acknowledged and Pentecost was celebrated). More than any other factor, it was the experience of wrestling with the crushing darkness of clinical depression that drew me to a more formal devotional life: when you really cannot pray yourself, when every form of 'felt' experience has fled, when you are despairing of yourself and despairing of God, then the prayers of others become precious. The psalms of lament, the prayers of Jeremiah, the prayers of Job, these all became my prayers. I was taken by surprise by the poetry of hymns I had sung unthinkingly for years. And I discovered prayers of the Church, some ancient and some contemporary,

---

[4] For a discussion of Spurgeon's understanding of the sacraments see Tim Grass and Ian Randall, 'C.H. Spurgeon on the Sacraments', in Anthony R. Cross and Philip E. Thompson (eds), *Baptist Sacramentalism* (Carlisle: Paternoster Press, 2003), pp. 55-75.

that expressed concisely and profoundly what I would have wanted to pray myself had I been able.

I came late, then, to a formal liturgy, to the saying of the daily office as the form of my 'quiet time'. And thereby I came late, but so gratefully, to the rhythm of the Christian Year: to canticles, collects, readings, and responses that draw you in to the unfolding Christian story; to the humbling sense of praying and worshipping in unison with the Church in its connectedness across the continents and across the ages. Without any compromise of my Baptist and Reformed convictions I became 'catholic', and it felt like coming home.

This practice of catholicity should not be underrated: in a context of radical individualism it is crucial for the Christian Church to be counter-cultural, or rather to intimate an alternative and transforming culture. Prayer and worship are never individual activities: we pray and worship before the Father, in the Son, and by the Spirit. When we come in the Lord's Prayer to say 'our Father...', we are participating together in Christ's praying; he invites us to join in his praying, and we pray together with him and with one another. The Lord's Prayer cannot be said in isolation. Worship and prayer occur in God, they are not things we do to God as over-against God. Worship and prayer are participatory: by the Spirit we are brought to participate in the Son's adoration of the Father and in the Son's eternal intercession before the Father; his praying includes our praying and our praying is included in his praying. And understood in this participatory sense, worship and prayer can never be individual acts; worship and prayer are necessarily corporate, necessarily ecclesial. When I pray my prayers, as participating in the praying of Christ by the Spirit, are simultaneously a participation in the praying of the Church. In prayer and in worship we join with the whole Church, in every place and in every age. In prayer and in worship we are joined with the Church in heaven as much as with the Church on earth. Notwithstanding our divisions we pray and worship as one—given that our worship and prayer occur only truly in Christ it could not be otherwise. And understood thus, while personal extempore prayers are to be encouraged, they are appropriately located in a liturgical context, in the context of worship and prayer that are authentically catholic, that represent the Church's worship and praying in its essential connectedness. To say the daily office, to follow the rhythm of the Christian Year, is to repudiate individualism and to confess our essential catholicity and corporateness.

But it is the underlying rhythm of this liturgical structure that forms the focus for this book. The seasons of the Christian Year are a liturgical unfolding of the Christian story and, as such, are a means of indwelling that story. The catholic creeds of the Church, to a significant degree, trace the narrative of the gospel: God is the creator of all things; the Son, who is of one essence with the Father, assumed our flesh and became human for our sake and for our salvation; he was born of the virgin Mary; he suffered under Pontius Pilate and was crucified; he rose from the dead on the third day; he ascended into heaven; he will come again in glory as our judge and his kingly reign will last forever; the Holy Spirit, who gives life to all things and who spoke through the prophets, has been sent by the Father and (or through) the Son; the Church is one, holy, catholic, and apostolic; there is a living communion with all God's holy people who one day will participate fully in the resurrection of Christ and in a life that is eternal. But, as has already been intimated, we too easily lose sight of this narrative structure and treat these creedal confessions as a series of abstracted (and often disconnected) propositions. And too easily these abstracted dogmatic propositions become the primary focus for our reflective attention, displacing the narratives to which they were, and can only ever be, a response. The Christian gospel is a narrative. The Word did not become text or a series of abstracted propositions; the Word became flesh (John 1.14). Consequently Christian theology, if it is to be done appropriately, must take the form of a sustained engagement with the story rather then merely an engagement with the Church's propositional responses to the story. And, since we come to know by indwelling rather than in detachment, Christian theology appropriately attempted will take the form of an indwelling of this story, being drawn into its dramas, identifying with its characterisations, tracing the movements of its plot. And since appropriate knowledge should be appropriate to its specific object, and since God is the object (or rather the irreducible subject) of theology,[5] this engagement with the gospel story which is the appropriate form of Christian theology is appropriately worshipful and prayerful.

And it is precisely this manner of worshipful and prayerful indwelling that is enabled by the liturgy of the Christian Year. Beginning with the affirmation of God as the one who comes (and who will come), the Church moves through the narrative of Christ's birth, of his baptism and revelation to the world, of his temptation and his journey to suffering and the Cross, of his resurrection and ascension, of his sending of the Spirit, and of his kingly reign together with all those made holy in him. Through prayers, canticles, readings, and responses the Church not only contemplates these stages of the story, it re-lives them, it enters into them, it is shaped by them. The Church journeys through the Christian Year with the Christ whose story is here narrated; the Church joins him in his journey and reaffirms his journey as its own journey, the journey by which it is defined and in which it participates. This is no detached

---

[5] For this understanding of God as the irreducible subject see in particular *CD* I/1, pp. 88-292 and II/1 pp. 179-254.

propositional dogmatics, this is a repetition and an indwelling of the story that is deeply engaging and inherently transformative. Through this liturgical cycle the Church reaffirms the story by which it is shaped and, accordingly, is shaped by that worshipful and prayerful indwelling. To celebrate the Christian Year is to engage in theological reflection that is narratival, doxological, and truly systematic.

There is, therefore, sound reason to structure an account of Christian dogmatics according to the seasons of the Christian Year. By its re-engagement with the elements of the Christian story itself such an approach should militate against the tendency to lose sight of the underlying story through a premature focus on propositions that are responsive to the story. By its sustained focus on the Christian story as that through which the living and true God is narrated to us such an approach should prove resistant to notions of God that are independent of this story and (very often) in tension with this story. And through its liturgical form such an approach to Christian dogmatics should never lose sight of the doxological and transformative character of authentic Christian theology.

It is far from easy, of course, to maintain this doxological character in any written study. The potential for artificiality is considerable. Anselm of Aosta (Bec and Canterbury) wrote his *Proslogion* as an extended prayer, addressing God throughout in the second person singular rather than speaking of God in the third person singular.[6] This is commendable but is hard to sustain and feels (and sounds) contrived to modern hearers and readers. The best I can attempt without artificiality is to begin and to end each chapter with an appropriate collect. I'm sure some readers will find this strategy insufficient and disappointing (given the more ambitious doxological aims stated above) and I will endeavour to write throughout in a more reflective and contemplative manner than is sometimes characteristic of systematic theologies. But ultimately a worshipful response to the gospel narrative cannot be imposed: it is a response of a reader or a writer; it cannot be enclosed or constrained within a text. All I can attempt is to set a study of God explicitly within the structure of a liturgical response to the gospel narrative, trusting the manner in which this text is received and heard to my readers and to the Spirit.

And if a doxological response to a text cannot be constrained or predicted then neither can an ethical response. A knowledge of the true and living God is inherently and inevitably transformative but while a text may be a means through which such transforming knowledge is imparted no text in and of itself has the power to impart such: here as elsewhere

---

⁶ Anselm, *Proslogion: Fides quaerens intellectum* (1077–78), trans. M.J. Charlesworth (Clarendon: Oxford, 1965).

this remains the prerogative of the Spirit. All a writer can do—and this I certainly try to do—is to make explicit the ethical commitment that is inherent and inevitable in any truthful knowledge of the true God. For the majority of Christian thinkers for the majority of the Church's history any distinction between the contemplation of doctrine and the disciplines of discipleship, between study and spirituality, would have been incomprehensible. Such a distinction, all too common in a contemporary context (and enshrined in so many Protestant courses in theology) is a disastrous instance of those disjunctions characteristic of the Enlightenment.[7] The knowledge of God is transformative; a confession of faith is a reorientation of life; belief is an ethical commitment.

A further instance of the disjunctions characteristic of the Enlightenment is the reduction of the ethical to the punctiliar: the study of ethics is reduced to the consideration of a series of supposedly discrete dilemmas, as if our human lives were disconnected and discontinuous, as if our decisions and actions were not outcomes of the continuity of our character and commitments. On the contrary, what we do is an outcome and outworking of who we are and the proper concern of Christian ethics is with the latter primarily and the former secondarily and derivatively. Traditionally this focus on character—on what we are called to become, on the manner in which we are being shaped through the Word and through the sacraments—has been explored through a consideration of the virtues, principally the three theological virtues (faith, hope, and love), and the four cardinal virtues (prudence, justice, temperance, and fortitude). The true goal of human life is communion with God, the beatific vision, and it is as we are formed in these virtues through the Word and the sacraments, through prayer and the spiritual disciplines, through our indwelling of the gospel story and our being indwelt by the Spirit, that we are fitted for this end.[8]

The tradition of the Church is far from unanimous in its numbering and identification of the seasons of the Christian Year: sometimes 'Ordinary Time' is listed as a separate 'season'; sometimes Pentecost is absorbed into the season of Easter, sometimes it is listed as a distinct season; sometimes 'Trinity' is listed as a distinct season; sometimes 'All Saints' Day' marks the beginning of a distinct 'Kingdom' season. For

---

[7] For an extended discussion of the relationship between Christian Doctrine and Christian Ethics see my book *Living the Christian Story: The Distinctiveness of Christian Ethics* (Edinburgh and New York: T & T Clark, 2001) or almost any work by Stanley Hauerwas, particularly *Character and the Christian Life: A Study in Theological Ethics* (Notre Dame and London: University of Notre Dame Press, 1994—originally published San Antonio: Trinity University Press, 1975) or *The Peaceable Kingdom: A Primer in Christian Ethics* (London: SCM Press, 1984).

[8] For the classic discussion of Christian virtues see the Prima Secundae and the Secunda Secundae of Thomas Aquinas' *Summa Theologiae*: *ST* I-II and II-II.

reasons of systematic and narratival development, but primarily in order to conform to my own devotional practice, I choose to follow the order of seasons listed in *Celebrating Common Prayer* as the discipline of the Society of Saint Francis.[9] Accordingly I move through Advent, Christmas, Epiphany, Lent, and Easter, celebrating Pentecost as a distinct season (including the longer period of 'Ordinary Time'), and allowing the celebration of 'All Saints' Day' to mark a distinctive 'Kingdom' season. Coincidentally, then, there are seven seasons of the Christian Year and there are seven virtues under which Christian character has generally been considered. Here the temptation to artificiality is irresistible. And it is artificiality: anticipating future criticisms I confess that the linking of these virtues with the seasons of the Christian Year is a convenience of systematic tidiness rather than a matter of any inherent association. The link between advent and hope, of course, is both traditional and coherent, but other associations are admittedly contrived and tenuous. I am not apologising for this, I am simply admitting it lest any reader assume an inherent connection that is not being implied or intended. What is intended, and what is being expressed by this admittedly artificial series of associations, is the ethical nature of doxological theology, the transformative outcome of any true indwelling of the gospel story. To celebrate this story is to participate in this story is to be shaped and transformed by this story. No re-telling of this story, therefore, should occur other than worshipfully, with the prayerful expectation that such transformation will occur, both in speaker and author and in listener and reader. My prayer, then, as I begin this journey is simply that it will prove to be a journey, an indwelling of the story that is effectively doxological and transformative.

> Glory be to the Father, and to the Son,
> and to the Holy Spirit:
> as it was in the beginning, is now,
> and shall be for ever.
> Amen.

---

[9] *Celebrating Common Prayer: A version of The Daily Office SSF*, The European Province of the Society of Saint Francis (London: Mowbray, 1992).

CHAPTER 1

The One Who Comes

Almighty God,
give us grace to cast away the works of darkness
and to put on the armour of light,
now in the time of this mortal life,
in which your Son Jesus Christ came to us in great humility:
so that on the last day,
when he shall come again in his glorious majesty
to judge the living and the dead,
we may rise to the life immortal;
through him who is alive and reigns with you and the Holy Spirit,
one God, now and for ever.
Amen.[1]

The season of Advent has a double reference, looking back to the prophetic anticipations of Christ's coming and looking forward to his final coming, as our judge, at the end of this age. At Advent, then, we begin at the end and end at the beginning, we look forwards by looking backwards and look backwards by looking forwards. We confess the provisionality of our present existence and understanding. We confess that we live in hope.

As the title suggests, the season of Advent directs our attention to God as the one who comes and identifies God as such. He is the one who has come and he is the one who will come. It is as the one who comes that God is related to us and to the universe. Towards the beginning of the book of Revelation, God, to and through the apostle, reveals himself as the Alpha and the Omega, as the one who is and who was and who is coming, as the one who is almighty (Revelation 1.8).[2] It may not be entirely inappropriate or fanciful to relate this self-identification of God at the end of the New Testament to God's self-identification to Moses at the burning bush (Exodus 3.14): when Moses asks concerning God's name God replies "I AM WHO I AM" (or possibly "I WILL BE WHO I

---

[1] *CCP*, p. 68; cf. *BCP*.
[2] Ἐγώ εἰμι τὸ Ἄλφα καὶ τὸ Ὦ, λέγει κύριος ὁ θεός, ὁ ὢν καὶ ὁ ἦν καὶ ὁ ἐρχόμενος, ὁ παντοκράτωρ.

WILL BE").[3] The imperfect tense in Hebrew (which is used here) conveys the sense of a continuing action, whether in the past, the present, or the future: hence God is who he always was, who he continues to be, who he will be; he is who he was as the God of Abraham, the God of Isaac, and the God of Jacob (v. 15); he is who he will be in the unfolding of his history with his people; he will not be manipulated by Moses or by anyone else; he will be who he will be.

For Thomas Aquinas the form of this self-identification by God to Moses was of foundational significance for the whole of theology: whereas even the term 'God' can only be applied to God analogically (since it can be applied also to that which is deemed, albeit falsely, to be 'god', and since it can be applied also to that which is brought to participate in God[4]), this self-identification of God as the one who is (*Qui est*) 'most properly belongs to God' since it signifies God's pure existence.[5] Thomas has been criticised by several twentieth-century scholars for placing so much weight on this text with scant regard for its historical context and significance: historically the narrative more probably and more simply refers to the impossibility and inappropriateness of any attempt to invoke God or to manipulate God; God as revealed to Moses is other than the 'gods' of the nations. But such dismissals, whether or not historically accurate, are theologically inept. Whatever the significance of this narrative may or may not have been to supposed original writers or original hearers (and how can anyone know such with such dogmatic certainty?) Thomas is entirely justified in identifying its theological significance beyond any immediate historical reference as ultimately defining God in distinction to all else that is not God: God alone simply 'is'.

Contrary to the assumptions of so many of his supposed theological heirs and so many more of his theological detractors, Thomas' concern in his discussion of the 'names' of God is not to propose a basis in analogy for a 'natural' theology, a means of speaking of God merely on the basis of created reality, an 'analogy of being' between God and creation (as Laurence Hemming observes, Thomas never employs the term '*analogia entis*').[6] Thomas' concern rather, and more simply, is to identify the meaningfulness of words when they are used with reference to God; even (and particularly) the meaningfulness of such words when used by God himself in the course of his self-revelation; Thomas' concern was to ensure that when we speak of God we speak of God truly;

---

[3] אהיה אשר אהיה.

[4] See John 10.34ff.

[5] *ST* I 13 10-11.

[6] Laurence Paul Hemming, '*Analogia non Entis sed Entitatis*: The Ontological Consequences of the Doctrine of Analogy', *IJST* 6/2 (2004), pp. 118-129.

Thomas' concern was to ensure that we understand the limitations of the words we use of God, and even of the words God uses of himself.

Our human words, of course, are always limited: our words can never be adequate for our concepts; I can never fully express to you the ideas, images, and feelings that I have in my mind. This is the nature and limitation of all human language whether written or spoken and, ultimately, it is irresolvable. The more thoroughly you know me, the more likely you are to understand me; the closer and more defined our community, the more effective our communication. As Scripture acknowledges more than once, only God truly knows us; only God fully understands the thoughts of our 'hearts'. But when our human words are used about God, even when God employs our human words to speak about himself, the matter is greatly compounded. How can human words ever be adequate to God? How can we possibly come to express the inexpressible? To grasp the gravity of this problem is to recognise and embrace the essential humility that should be characteristic of all theological language. Consequently, John Calvin (following Athanasius, Thomas Aquinas, and others) speaks of God accommodating himself to human language, employing our human words in all their limitations as means and instruments of his revelation albeit provisionally and partially.[7] And ultimately the Word, the eternal Son of God, becomes flesh because mere words, mere text, mere language, can never be enough.

But even when we have grasped this general inadequacy of words to concepts, together with this particular and inevitable inadequacy of words when referring to God, we have only begun to engage with the difficulty since (and this is the point which Thomas makes with such clarity and force) words when applied to God, even when applied by God to God, take on rather different significance to that of their common use. Take the simple verb 'to be' for instance: when we say that any created thing 'is' we are referring to its created and therefore dependent and contingent existence; but when we say that God, the creator, 'is' we are referring to God's uncreated and therefore non-dependent and non-contingent existence; we are, in some respects, saying the opposite of what we were saying when we were referring to the existence of creatures. We are not saying the complete opposite, of course; in both respects we are referring to existence, albeit very different existence; we are not using the word 'is' equivocally. But neither are we using the word 'is' univocally; we are not saying precisely the same thing, we are, in fact, saying a rather different (though related) thing; we are using the word 'is' analogously.

And what is true of this simple word 'is' is true inevitably of every other word (and phrase): juxtapose any word (or phrase) to the word

---

[7] *Institutes* I xvii 13.

'God' and its significance is altered; human words can only be used of God analogously, even when God himself uses them. The forgetfulness of this most basic characteristic of religious language lies at the root of so much theological error, confusion, and foolishness. Take the word 'cause' as an example of such confusion. As soon as we start thinking of God's causality and creaturely causality as simply and essentially the same dynamic these two causalities become mutually limiting: the more causality we accord to God the less can be accorded to the creature; the more causality we accord to the creature the less can be accorded to God. And so we slip into interminable, irresolvable, and utterly pointless arguments about divine sovereignty and human freedom, not realising that the entire debate rests on the mistaken assumption that divine causality and creaturely causality are continuous, are essentially the same dynamic. But as Thomas Aquinas, John Calvin, Jonathan Edwards, and Karl Barth all recognise (albeit rather differently), divine causality is quite different to creaturely causality, indeed, divine causality is the ground and possibility of creaturely causality rather than its threat or rival.[8]

But returning to the point in question, God exists in a manner quite different from any other reality: God exists uniquely as the creator, all else exists as God's creation; God exists independent of all other reality, all other reality exists in dependence on God; there is a sense, therefore, in which only God truly 'is'; God is the one who 'is'; he is the 'I am'. Moreover (and I hope without tautology), God 'is' as the one he is, as the one whose existence is uniquely non-dependent; God is self-existent; his existence is self-determined; he is who he is ('I will be who I will be'). And the season of Advent, in response to the text at the beginning of the book of Revelation and echoing the witness of Scripture from beginning to end, identifies this uniquely self-existent God as the one who comes. This simple affirmation is pregnant with significance for God's relatedness to all that is not God: it affirms the freedom of God's immanence; it affirms the freedom of his relatedness to his creation. That God comes to his creation identifies God as other than his creation, albeit as the one who comes to his creation. And God comes to his creation as the one he is, and as the one he was—here is an affirmation of the freedom of God's constancy alongside the affirmation of the constancy of his freedom.

God is simple. He is undivided. His nature is single and singular. His perfections (or attributes), therefore, are not in tension; the various perfections of God are merely the inevitably various and partial ways we have of speaking and responding to God's single, undivided nature. Consequently, God's freedom and God's constancy are mutually

---

[8] *ST* I 22; *Institutes* I xvi; Jonathan Edwards, *YE* 18 *The "Miscellanies" 501-832*, ed. Ava Chamberlain, Entry 629, p. 157; *CD* III/3, pp. 94-107.

informing rather than tensions in God's nature and to overlook this mutuality again issues inevitably in distortion. Other than as informed by the divine constancy God's freedom can be misconstrued as divine arbitrariness. Other than as informed by the divine freedom God's constancy can be misconstrued as an impersonal and static immobility. And since, in the Western tradition at least, these divine perfections have all too often been so misconstrued, it is hardly surprising that they have consequently been qualified or even repudiated.

Colin Gunton opines that from Augustine onwards the Western tradition has tended to misconstrue God's freedom as arbitrariness, has failed to inform the affirmation of God's freedom with the corresponding affirmation of God's personal constancy as the triune God who comes to his creation.[9] Accordingly God's transcendence has too often been conceived as the opposite of his immanence rather than as the form (and freedom) of his immanence; as his absolute (and static) otherness to the world rather than as the freedom of his personal and living immanence to the world. And whenever God's transcendence is misconstrued as a static and impersonal otherness it is hardly surprising that some, in order to affirm God's immanence, effectively deny his transcendence altogether.[10] But to deny the freedom of God's immanence to creation is to render creation, in some respects at least, necessary to God. And if creation is, in some respects, necessary to God then God is no longer God alone, creation itself participates in God's nature and in God's eternity: to undermine the freedom of God's immanence to creation is to undermine the distinct existence both of God and of creation; to undermine the freedom of God's immanence to creation is to undermine the aseity of God (his absolute sufficiency in himself; his absolute self-existence) and the contingent existence of creation (creation's dependent but distinct identity and integrity). The God of panentheism (or pantheism) cannot 'come' to creation since the distinction between God and creation has already been blurred if not abolished; if the world is already identified with God, or as a part or aspect of God, it is meaningless to speak of God's 'coming' to the world. Moreover, to conceive of God's immanence as necessary rather than free (or transcendent) is to forfeit any meaningful concept of divine grace—love that is necessary and inevitable is no longer freely loving;

---

[9] See for instance Colin E. Gunton, *The One, The Three and the Many: God, Creation and the Culture of Modernity*, The Bampton Lectures 1992 (Cambridge: Cambridge University Press, 1993), pp. 120-21.

[10] For examples of tendencies in this direction see the 'process theology' of Charles Hartshorne in *Man's Vision of God and the Logic of Theism* (New York: Harper, 1941), or the feminist panentheistic theology of Sally MacFague in *The Body of God: An Ecological Theology* (London: SCM Press, 1993).

that God 'comes' to his creation is an act of grace and the act of coming itself, as a free act, identifies God as gracious.

The season of Advent, the text at the beginning of the book of Revelation, and the narrative of Christian Scripture as a whole witness to God as the one who freely comes to his creation. He is not identical to his creation nor does creation participate in his being and nature. As the one who remains entirely self-existent, as the one who never becomes dependent upon his creation, but as the one who grants creation its distinct though contingent existence and integrity, God freely comes to his creation. And God freely comes to his creation as the one he freely is, as the one whose coming to his creation is not a necessity of his nature, but also as the one whose coming to his creation is not a contradiction of his nature (and, in this sense, whose coming is unsurprising). God comes to his creation as the one he is and as the one he was.

In the narrative of the burning bush God identifies himself to Moses as the one who is, but he also identifies himself to Moses as 'the God of your fathers' as 'the God of Abraham, the God of Isaac and the God of Jacob'; as the one who was; as the one identified by this name 'from generation to generation' (Exodus 3.15). The one who comes to Moses is the one who came to Abraham, to Isaac, and to Jacob, and from generation to generation he will be who he is and who he was. As this living and personal one (rather than as some static and impersonal abstraction) God is eternally constant, eternally faithful. The vision granted to John on Patmos, the vision of God as the one 'who is, and who was, and who is to come' is, at the same time, a vision of the risen and exalted Christ; a vision of one who was dead and is now alive for ever (Revelation 1.18); a vision of one who yet bears the marks of slaughter (Revelation 5.6). The God who comes to his creation, therefore, is the one who is as he has been beforehand in his history with his people and ultimately in the gospel story, in the Son's taking flesh and dwelling amongst us in the power of the Spirit. And the one he was in this history, in the gospel story, is the one he is now and always was and always will be. He is changeless throughout the ages and in eternity as this living and personal one, as the God narrated in the gospel story.

God's self-disclosure to Moses at the burning bush, then, is not quite the enigmatic philosophical abstraction it is sometimes mistakenly assumed to be. It is content-full. God here identifies himself as the one who was known by Abraham, Isaac, and Jacob and who, therefore, can be known through these stories of his engagement with these three very different people. And they were very different people: preachers sometimes comment (perhaps too simplistically) that men like Abraham tend to have sons like Isaac, and that men like Isaac tend to have sons like Esau and Jacob—be that as it may, the book of Genesis narrates the story of God's very different relating to these very different men, and, yet, notwithstanding the diversity of their personalities as rendered here, and the consequent differences in the manner of God's relating to them, he remains constant in these three very different relationships. I love my son no more and no less than I love my daughter, and I love my daughter no more and no less than I love my son, but I cannot relate to them in the same way, they are two such different people. Abraham, Isaac, and Jacob are different, God relates to them personally and particularly and therefore differently; but through these differences of relating he remains constant, he remains the one who is utterly faithful to his covenant, he remains the same. And as the one known through these personal and particular relationships he makes himself known to Moses. This is who he is. This is who he will be. This is his name throughout the generations.

And as the story of God's personal relatedness to Moses unfolds, and as the subsequent story of his relatedness to Israel unfolds through the stories of his personal relatedness to Israel's judges, to Israel's kings, to Israel's priests, to Israel's prophets, and to so many individual characters in this unfolding story, Hebrew and non-Hebrew, women and men, so the nature and being of this utterly constant God is narrated to us, not just in narrative itself, but also in poems and songs and prophecies and proverbs and laws, all of which assume an underlying narrative and emerge from it. The changelessness of God narrated here is certainly not the changelessness of the static and immobile abstraction of Aristotelian philosophy—God is narrated here as living and personal, interacting with his people, coming to his creation. The changelessness of God narrated here is rather the changelessness of utter faithfulness, of living and personal constancy. In his coming to his people and to his creation God is constantly who he always was and always will be. And through these stories, poems, songs, prophecies, proverbs, and laws the nature and being of God is narrated, but never with a sense of completion, always prophetically pregnant with a future, always anticipating that the one who has come to his people will come again and again to his people, that prophecy will be fulfilled, that shadow will give way to reality.

Traditionally during the season of Advent we reflect upon the witnesses to the coming Christ—the prophets, John the Baptist, Mary—these are lights (among so many other lights) pointing to the decisive and definitive coming of God in Christ. But who God is in Christ is not contrary to or even in tension with who he was to and through these anticipatory lights. Who he is in Christ is who he truly always was. Who he was in this prophetic and anticipatory history is now identified in this decisive and definitive coming.

In the past God spoke to our ancestors through the prophets at many times and in various ways, but in these last days he has spoken to us by his Son, whom he appointed heir of all things, and through whom he made the universe. The Son is the radiance of God's glory and the exact representation of his being, sustaining all

things by his powerful word. After he had provided purification for sins, he sat
down at the right hand of the Majesty in heaven. (Hebrews 1.1-3)

That this God who comes to us subsists as Father, Son, and Holy Spirit is
disclosed in the gospel story. The gospel story, as Jürgen Moltmann and
others have observed, is not simply the story of Jesus but the story of
Jesus in personal relation to his Father and in personal relation to the
Holy Spirit.[11] The passage from the beginning of the Letter to the
Hebrews identifies the Son who takes our flesh as the full expression of
the Father's subsistence (a term that would assume vast significance in the
trinitarian debates of the Early Church),[12] and, in subsequent verses
(especially vv. 10-12), passages from the Old Testament that refer simply
and explicitly to God himself are applied without qualification or
explanation to Christ. And the Holy Spirit, who is received by the Son
from the Father and sent upon and among his Church (Acts 2.33), is
identified in the Fourth Gospel as 'another Counsellor',[13] another one
like Christ himself, to be with us for ever (John 14.16).

However, the point at issue here is not to establish that the Son and the
Spirit are truly God, of one essence with the Father and sharing his glory
(though this is the irreducible core of the faith of the Church): too often
such attempted demonstrations assume a notion of God derived from
somewhere other than the gospel and consequently struggle to make the
one disclosed in the gospel conform to these preconceptions. The point at
issue is rather (and on the contrary) to infer rather than to deduce: to
conclude from the gospel story that God truly is the one who is revealed
here as Father, Son, and Spirit; that the one who comes here is the one
who is and who always was; that God is truly as he is in Christ and in the
Spirit rather than just that Christ and the Spirit are truly God. The
Christian Church confesses that God has defined himself in the gospel
story; that who God is here he is eternally; that the one true God subsists
eternally as the Father, the Son, and the Spirit; that the one who made
himself known to Abraham, Isaac, and Jacob, to Moses and Aaron, to the
prophets, priests, and kings of Israel and Judah, is and always was truly
this triune God.

The doctrine of the Trinity, therefore, together with the doctrine of
Christ's true deity and true humanity, is that which makes the Christian
Church 'Christian', is that which distinguishes the Christian Church from
Judaism and from Islam, is that which identifies what the Christian Church
means when it utters the word 'God'. The one who comes in this story is
the one who is truly and eternally God. And as Augustine of Hippo and

---

[11] Jürgen Moltmann, *The Trinity and the Kingdom of God: The Doctrine of God*, trans.
Margaret Kohl (London: SCM Press, 1981), pp. 61-96.
[12] ὅς ὣς ἀπαύγασμα τῆς δόξης καὶ χαρακτὴρ τῆς ὑποστάσεως αὐτου...
[13] ἄλλον παράκλητον.

others have contended,[14] this triune identification of God could not be more significant and distinctive: the doctrine of the Trinity enables the Christian Church to confess the true God as eternally and freely loving.[15] That God subsists eternally as Father, Son, and Spirit enables the confession that God is eternally loving in himself without and before creation. A notion of God as solely and simply 'one' (a monistic notion of God) either would issue in a notion of God as indeterminate arbitrary will (since there would be nothing eternally in or alongside God as the object of love, nothing eternally in or alongside God to render his will determinate rather than indeterminate and arbitrary), or would issue in a notion of a loving God whose love eternally was dependent upon there being a creation, something other than God, as the object of God's eternal love (but, as was noted previously, a creation that is necessary to God renders God no longer God alone; a creation that is necessary to God is no longer the outcome of a gracious and free act of God; and a love for creation that is eternally necessary if God is to be conceived as eternally loving is no longer a love that is truly free and gracious). The Church's identification of the one true God as Father, Son, and Spirit (in response to the gospel story) is, therefore, that which enables the Church to confess God as eternally loving (without there being a creation for him to love), creation as a free act of this loving God (unnecessitated by the confession of God as eternally loving), and God's love for creation as free and gracious (again unnecessitated by the confession of God as eternally loving).

While superficially the doctrine of the Trinity may appear to conflict with a notion of divine simplicity it rather, in fact, enables a doctrine of the simplicity of this, the true God. The doctrine of divine simplicity, as mentioned previously and as expounded by Thomas Aquinas amongst others,[16] attests that God, in order truly to be 'God', must be 'simple' in the sense of not being complex; he is undivided, he simply 'is'. Since God is who he is constantly, since he is who he was and who he always will be, there can be no division in God, no change in God, no 'potential' in God of his being other than who he is since who he is he is eternally and constantly. At a superficial level, then, the doctrine of the Trinity, the confession of God's threeness as the Father, the Son, and the Spirit, would appear to conflict with this notion of simplicity: if God by nature is simple and undivided how can he be Father, Son, and Spirit? But the

---

[14] Aurelius Augustine, *On the Holy Trinity* in *NPNF*1, vol. 3 (Grand Rapids and Edinburgh: Eerdmans and T & T Clark, 1993), pp. 17-228.

[15] For a more sustained discussion of the doctrine of the Trinity and of the merits and demerits of Augustine's contribution to our understanding of the doctrine see my earlier work *Promise and Presence: An Exploration of Sacramental Theology* (Milton Keynes: Paternoster, 2005), ch. 1.

[16] *ST* I 3.

simplicity attested by Thomas Aquinas and others is not the simplicity of some philosophical abstraction; it is the simplicity of this, the true and only God who has revealed himself in the gospel story (those who dismiss Thomas' work as an exercise in philosophical abstraction tend to take inadequate note that he begins his *Summa Theologiae* with a discussion of sacred doctrine and that this then forms the foundation for all that follows).[17] The true God who is simple, undivided, and unchanging is precisely the one who has revealed himself in the gospel story as the Father, the Son, and the Spirit. Moreover, this threeness of God (properly understood) does not imply any division in God but is rather the form of his oneness. Father, Son, and Holy Spirit are not divisions in God or parts of God: the single and undivided essence of God subsists fully, singly, and undividedly in the persons of the Father, Son, and Holy Spirit and in the mutual relations between these persons that constitute their distinct identities. It is, then, precisely as Father, Son, and Holy Spirit that the single and singular essence of God is simple and undivided.

Furthermore, only since the simple and undivided essence of God subsists simply and undividedly in the persons of the Father, the Son, and the Spirit and in the mutual relations between them can this simple and undivided essence be identified as determinate rather than indeterminate will, as eternal and unchanging love. The simplicity and changelessness of the true God who subsists as Father, Son, and Spirit is the simplicity and changelessness of the love mediated by the Spirit between the Father and the Son eternally. 'God is love' (1 John 4.16); 'God is light; in him there is no darkness at all' (1 John 1.5); God is not indeterminate, he is determinate; God is not arbitrary will, he is love—the love that binds Father, Son, and Spirit together in eternal, unchanging communion. This and this alone is the true simplicity of the true God; a simplicity issuing from God's triunity rather than the denial of it.[18]

To confess that God is 'almighty', therefore, is not to imply that he can do just anything, Scripture notes a number of things that God cannot do: he cannot change (Malachi 3.6); he cannot deny himself (2 Timothy 2.13); he cannot lie (Titus 1.2); his freedom is the determinate freedom to be the one he is; to be the one who eternally subsists as Father, Son, and Spirit; to be the one who is eternal love; he is not free to be other than himself. This non-freedom of God, of course, is not any form of external constraint: there can be nothing beyond God that can determine God's being and nature in any respect whatsoever; God is utterly free with respect to everything that is other than himself; God is utterly free with respect to creation; that God creates and loves his creation is an

---

[17] *ST* I 1.

[18] For an excellent discussion of divine simplicity see Stephen R. Holmes, *Listening to the Past: The Place of Tradition in Theology* (Carlisle: Paternoster Press, 2002), pp. 50-67.

utterly free, unconstrained, and gracious act. But God is not free from internal constraint—or, to put the matter positively, God is self-determined, he is constant, he is faithful. At the beginning of the second volume of his *Dogmatics*, Karl Barth identifies God as the 'One who Loves in Freedom' and from here onwards in his work this remains his underlying definition of the word 'God': as the one who loves God is and remains the one who is utterly and uniquely free, but this freedom is his freedom rather than some anonymous freedom, it is the determinate freedom of his love rather than the indeterminate freedom of an arbitrary will; God is free but God is not capricious.[19] The doctrine of God's simplicity and changelessness, therefore, constitutes a constraint and limitation on God, or rather, a constraint and limitation within God: he is who he was; he cannot be other than he eternally is; and he eternally is who he has revealed himself to be in his coming to us in the gospel story.

Nor does God's coming to us in the gospel story imply any change in his being, any qualification of his simplicity. He comes to us as the one he eternally is, or rather, he eternally is as he is in his coming to us. He is not in any way constrained, either internally or externally, to come to that which is other than himself; that he comes to that which is other than himself is an entirely gracious and unconstrained act. But that he comes to that which is other than himself, while an entirely gracious and unconstrained act, is not an incoherent act: his coming to us does not change or modify his eternal being and nature; his coming to us is a reiteration of his eternal being and nature; it is precisely as he eternally is and was that he comes to us.[20] The true God is perfectly loving in himself in all eternity in the perfect communion of the Father, the Son, and the Spirit—God does not need there to be a universe in order to be loving in himself—but that God creates the universe, loves the universe, and comes to the universe, is entirely coherent with his eternal and self-existent nature, though not in anyway constrained by that nature or by any other factor. He comes to us as the one who is and was without us. His coming to us is a gracious reiteration of the lovingness which is his eternal being and nature as Father, Son, and Spirit.

God is and was, then, who he is in his coming and he will be, in his coming, who he is and was. As has already been noted, the vision granted to John on Patmos of the risen and exalted Christ is yet the vision of the one who is 'Son of Man', one who continues to bear the wounds of the Cross. The one who will come is not other than the one who came; he will be who he was and is. Too commonly we fail to notice the rhetoric of this book of Revelation (not to mention the rhetorical force of so many other

---

[19] *CD* II/1, pp. 257-321.

[20] For this notion of revelation as reiteration see Eberhard Jüngel, *The Doctrine of the Trinity: God's Being is in Becoming*, trans. Horton Harris (Edinburgh: Scottish Academic Press, 1976), pp. 89ff.

passages of Scripture). A vision of the glorified Christ is a vision of one 'like a son of man' (Revelation 1.13); the 'Lion of the tribe of Judah', the 'Root of David' who 'has triumphed', proves to be a 'Lamb, looking as if it had been slain' (5.5-6.); the worship that is offered to the one seated on the throne is offered to this Lamb; the great dragon who is cast out of heaven is overcome by 'the blood of the Lamb' and by the 'word' of the testimony of those who lay down their lives in faithfulness (12.7-11); the rider of a white horse who comes to judge and to make war with justice strikes the nations with a sword that comes out of his mouth (19.11-16). The one who will come is not other than the one who came. This is not some strange Jesus. Worldly images of majesty, power, and violence are consistently and systematically deconstructed. He comes to judge, but he comes to judge justly. He comes to conquer, but he conquers as the Lamb who was slain. At the end of this age Christ does not resort to the worldly violence and power he once rejected—to fail to recognise this is to fail to recognise the rhetoric of this vision—at the end of this age Christ comes as the slaughtered Lamb and conquers by his word. He comes as the one he ever is and ever was.

And therefore, in the season of Advent and as always, we can face the future with confidence rather than anxiety; we can face the future with hope; we know who is coming. The one who came is the one who comes and he will come as the one he is and was eternally.

To speak of 'hope', of course, implies a 'not yet'; notwithstanding the actuality of the gospel story, of the reality of God's coming to us and to his creation, the past and the present are marked by provisionality in every respect, the history of redemption has not yet reached its conclusion, we live in hope. 'The Word became flesh and made his dwelling among us…'—nothing can qualify this truth or detract from it (and we will explore its significance more fully in succeeding chapters); '[w]e have seen his glory, the glory of the One and Only…'—yes, we have seen, but not all have seen, and those who have seen have not fully comprehended (John 1.14). For the present 'we know in part and we prophesy in part' (1 Corinthians 13.9), what we presently see is 'but a poor reflection in a mirror' (13.12); the day will come when, finally, 'we shall see face to face', but that day is not yet here and to think or act as if it were here is great foolishness and the root of appalling error.

There have always been (and are still) those who speak and act as if they already fully knew and fully comprehended, those who seemingly present their systems of theology with a confidence bordering on arrogance, as if their responses to the gospel constituted a final word of unequalled clarity (conversely Karl Barth, reportedly, was relieved and grateful that his massive *Church Dogmatics* remained unfinished; Thomas Aquinas refused to complete his *Summa Theologiae*). There have been (and are still) Protestants who misconstrue and misappropriate a notion of

Scripture's inspiration and perspicuity, assuming the Bible itself to be the perfection of revelation (with no notion of the limitations of human language discussed previously), bestowing on Scripture the place and title that belong properly and solely to Christ, and wallowing in the delusion that their reading of Scripture is immediate, direct, unimpaired, and certain. The prayers and reflections of Advent, then, should compel us to humility and a proper hesitancy. The 'already' of God's coming to us is qualified by the 'not yet' of his future and final coming. We do not yet see and hear as we shall then see and hear. We do not yet comprehend as we shall then comprehend—though even now 'angels long to look into these things' (1 Peter 1.12) and maybe even in the glory that is to come we will marvel but not fully comprehend (God will still be the creator and we will still be his creatures); when we fully know we shall realise how little we understand. We live in hope, not sight. A theology formed through Advent will always be marked by humility, caution, and a proper hesitancy.

To speak and live in hope signifies similarly that the kingdoms of this world have not yet become the kingdom of our God and of his Christ (though Christ's exaltation already clarifies the limitation of their contingent authority and repudiates any assumption of autonomy or ultimacy).[21] Christian hope is for a kingdom that is coming rather than a kingdom that has already come (at least in its fullness). Certainly Christians hope for penultimate comings of that kingdom, for provisional indications of God's name being hallowed, of his kingly reign being effected, of his will being done—but the ultimate coming of that kingdom lies in the future and the Church must never confuse the already with the not yet, the provisional with the ultimate. The kingdom of God must never be confused with all too human (and delusory) utopias, nor should Christians ever give way to the beguiling temptation to promote God's kingdom by all too human means, for to do so would be to apostatise and, implicitly, to blaspheme. This, of course, was the principal failing of (so-called) Christendom: when the Church found itself in a position of prominence and influence the temptation to use the means of violence and coercion to promote its ends (though it may simultaneously have blurred its vision of its true ends) proved too great. But by employing such means and, worse still, by seeking to justify those means theologically, the Church denied its true Master by justifying what he repudiates and implicitly proclaimed a notion of God's nature entirely contrary to that nature as defined in the gospel story. The Christ who comes is the Christ who came, is the one who repudiated violent

---

[21] For a provocative discussion of the significance of Christ's exaltation (and a compelling defence of the notion of Christendom) see Oliver O'Donovan, *The Desire of the Nations: Rediscovering the Roots of Political Theology* (Cambridge: Cambridge University Press, 1996).

retaliation, is the one who went passively to the Cross, praying forgiveness for those who tortured him. One cannot coherently torture a prisoner, fight a crusade, or burn a heretic in the name of this Christ. The Christendom of the medieval and early-modern Western Church, of course, is not the sole instance of such apostasy: whenever any 'Christian' sect mistakes the penultimate for the ultimate and adopts means that are inappropriate to its true ends Christ is denied and God's name is taken in vain. We live in hope, and theology shaped by Advent will not be beguiled into confusing the penultimate with the ultimate or employing means that are a denial of authentically gospel ends.

To confuse the penultimate with the ultimate, to be beguiled by human utopias, is a quite astonishing delusion in the light of the gravity and universality of the symptoms of penultimacy with which we are constantly confronted. All around us creation is groaning and we are groaning with it:

> We know that the whole creation has been groaning as in the pains of childbirth right up to the present time. Not only so, but we ourselves, who have the first-fruits of the Spirit, groan inwardly as we wait eagerly for our adoption, the redemption of our bodies. For in this hope we were saved. But hope that is seen is no hope at all. Who hopes for what one already has? But if we hope for what we do not yet have, we wait for it patiently. (Romans 8.22-25)

Earlier in this passage Paul has spoken of the whole creation as being 'subjected to frustration', being in 'bondage to decay' (vv. 20-21), and the ubiquity of decadence and frustration is overwhelming. Daily we hear reports of wars and rumours of wars; daily we hear reports of famine, flood, earthquake or volcanic eruption. This chapter is being written in the aftermath of terrorist attacks in London, a tornado in Birmingham, drought and famine in Niger, floods in India, unimaginable violence and terror in Iraq, the uncovering of a disturbingly extensive network of child abuse in an area of France, alongside the 'usual' instances of rape, murder, robbery, and corruption. The world presently hovers on the edge of environmental disaster and ideological conflict. And in any season the catalogue of suffering would prove depressingly similar. Some utopia! Creation and we within it are simply not yet as God ultimately wills. But because we know that the one who came will come we do not give way to despair; we live in hope. Theology that is formed through the prayers and reflections of Advent will never seek to belittle or to minimise the frustrations and decadence of present existence, but theology shaped in Advent will never be overwhelmed by those marks of frustration and decadence nor will it succumb to unremitting despair; theology formed through Advent will hope and that hope will echo prophetically in a world of futility and violence. Stanley Hauerwas speaks of optimism as 'hope without truth':[22] a theology of Advent will not subscribe to false optimisms (though it is hard not to be both impressed and baffled by the dogged resilience of political optimisms in the context of such crises and tragedies); a theology of Advent confronts the truth of creation's present bondage to decay with the truth of its prospective liberation, its participation in the glorious freedom of the children of God; a theology of Advent expresses itself in hope.

To live hopefully is certainly not to live negligently or carelessly. This world may be in bondage to decay but it remains God's world, the arena of his covenant love; it is he who has subjected it and he has subjected it in hope (none other could subject the world 'in hope'). Moreover, the hope of creation is to participate in the 'glorious freedom of the children of God': it is not unreasonable, therefore, for the children of God, here and now, to be mediators of that freedom, albeit penultimately. To live in hope is to acknowledge that ultimate freedom lies in the future, but to live in hope is to anticipate penultimate signs of this ultimate freedom and to be the means of such. The Church may not be able to avert environmental disaster—such is an inherent symptom of this world's present bondage—but the Church will live responsibly and thereby prophetically, indicating by a manner of living and speaking both the reality and depth of this present bondage and the possibility and prospect of penultimate as well as ultimate liberation. The Church, at least of itself, may not be able to 'make poverty history'—poverty also is an inherent mark of present bondage—but the Church in this respect also can live responsibly and thereby prophetically, anticipating ultimate liberation by penultimate acts of justice, mercy, and uncalculating generosity.

And to speak and live hopefully is to confront more personal futilities with the truth of the gospel story. It is not just the world but we ourselves within it who are not yet as God would ultimately have us to be and will make us. Though daily we are being shaped by the mediated Word of God and by the sacramental life of the Church this work of spiritual re-birth, this continuing work of sanctification as the Holy Spirit persists with us, has not yet reached its completion. Daily we are beset with the memory of past sins and both depressed and oppressed by the persistence of the temptations and disordered loves that gave birth to such. Daily we are amazed at our own continuing capacity for depravity and even more amazed at the constancy of divine mercy and grace that continues to grasp us when our grasp falters. With respect to the coherence and consistency of our discipleship and spirituality we certainly do not live by 'sight', but we live in hope. We know that the one who comes is yet the one who came for our forgiveness and cleansing. We know that the mercy

---

[22] Stanley Hauerwas, *Christian Existence Today: Essays on Church, World, and Living In Between* (Durham, NC: Labyrinth, 1988), p. 211.

and grace revealed and actualised in his Cross and resurrection will not allow our sin, frailty, and corruption to be the last word. We know that the one who began this work within us 'will carry it on to completion until the day of Christ Jesus' (Philippians 1.6). And so in this respect too we live in hope, not overwhelmed by our sin and our propensity to sin, but continually trusting in a mercy that forgives and a grace that restores and transforms. We live and worship as those whose true present identity is located in the future, 'hidden with Christ in God' (Colossians 3.3), rather than in the past.

Moreover we live in hope not just with respect to our spiritual malaise but also our physical demise. We are ageing: our sight dims, our hearing fails, our steps falter, our strength diminishes, and our memory fades. Despite the progress of medical science there is little we can do to check the advances of cancer, heart failure, arthritis, or dementia. And ultimately there is nothing we can do to halt this demise. We know that we shall die and the prospect of death haunts so many as the ultimate mocking of all that has been, as the concluding triumph of meaninglessness. But in the context of this demise and the prospect of this death we live in hope. Because we believe that the one who came is the one who is coming, that the one who died and who rose is the one who is our future, we hope beyond the grave. Our prospect is not a rotting cadaver but the resurrection of the body and the life everlasting. The hopefulness that is formed through a theology of Advent is not trivial or superficial; it is not forgetful or belittling of the inevitability of demise and death but neither is it wholly overwhelmed by this inevitability.

Advances in medical science, though bringing incalculable benefits to human society, also issue in ultimately false optimism. For all that such advances have achieved there is so much more that has not been achieved and possibly will never be achieved, and ultimately we all will die: the death rate is now and has always been one hundred percent. Knowing this, the Christian must never be beguiled into mistaking the penultimate hope of present healing for the ultimate hope of resurrection. To live by this ultimate hope is not to seek to cling to this present life at all costs; it is to face sickness, dying, and death reluctantly but also peacefully and hopefully. And it is to face sickness, dying, and death; it is not ultimately to seek to evade such or avoid such. To live hopefully is to know that, here and now, sickness, dying, and death cannot ultimately be evaded or avoided. And to live hopefully issues in a commitment to care for one another even when there is little prospect of cure (and there is never an ultimate prospect of cure). Indeed, to live hopefully is never to allow the possibility of penultimate cure to deflect or to diminish the responsibility to care. The hopefulness that is formed through a theology of Advent cannot evade grief and pain but it persists through such; it is a candle that cannot be extinguished.

Such a hope as this, of course, can never be a merely private affair: it is a hope for the individual Christian, but it is also the hope of the whole Church, and the hope of the world. Indeed, finally it is the only hope for the world even though the world may not yet know it or share it. The hope of the New Testament is unequivocally universal: there is no reality that is not destined to be brought to completion in Christ; there is no knee that will not bow to him, no tongue that will not confess him; God may have bound all over to disobedience, but only so that 'he may have mercy on them all' (Romans 11.32). Such universal hope ought not to be confused with cheap universalism: the precise outworking of God's merciful love is not to be predicted or presumed upon; he may love men and women in such a manner as to allow their rejection of his mercy to remain eternally determinative; he may love men and women in such a manner as not to do so. But in either case this will be an outworking of his merciful love rather than its opposite for he has and is no opposite; he is who he was; he is simple and undivided; his justice is coherent with his love and not its contradiction; as Father, Son, and Spirit he is eternally loving not arbitrary. But while the merciful love of God can never be presumed upon or its outcomes predicted the hope that is formed by a theology of Advent can only be inclusive and never exclusive; a hope for the world and for all creation; a hope for all men and women; a hope for the Church and a hope for ourselves.[23]

Colin Gunton used to comment that the word 'hopefully' was probably the most misused adverb in the English language: we tend to speak of 'hopefully' doing something when we mean to signify that we hope we will do it rather than that we do it 'full of hope'. In a world so characterised by empty optimism and, consequently, by cynicism and despair, truly to live 'full of hope' is radically distinctive, is itself a prophetic witness. Simply by its hopefulness, the Christian Church—shaped by the prayers and reflections of Advent, indwelling the expectancy of the Old Testament and the continuing expectancy of the New, awaiting the coming of the one who came, the one who is who he was—will live and speak prophetically within a world otherwise devoid of authentic hope. Such a Church will constantly be aware of what it isn't as much as of what it is and will be; of its provisionality as much of its actuality. Such a Church will live and speak hopefully.

---

[23] Some theological texts are so brilliant that, no matter how hard you try to think and to write freshly and independently, they utterly shape your thinking and your writing. Throughout this discussion of Christian hope, then, I gladly and gratefully admit my indebtedness to and inevitable dependence upon Karth Barth's discussion of the theme in chapter 73 of his *Dogmatics*: *CD* IV/3, pp. 902-42.

O God, by whose command
the order of time runs its course:
forgive our restlessness, perfect our faith
and, while we await the fulfilment of your promise,
grant us to have a good hope
through the Word made flesh,
even Jesus Christ our Lord.
Amen.[24]

---

[24] *CCP*, p. 79, and Ven. David Silk *Prayers for Use at the Alternative Services* (London: Mowbray, 1980).

CHAPTER 2

The One Who Takes Our Humanity

Almighty God,
who wonderfully created us in your own image
and yet more wonderfully restored us in your Son Jesus Christ:
grant that, as he came to share our human nature,
so we may be partakers in his divine glory;
who is alive and reigns with you and the Holy Spirit,
one God, now and for ever.
Amen.[1]

Even in the multi-ethnic, multi-cultural, pluralistic, and largely post-Christian society that is contemporary Britain the season of Christmas remains the one element of the Christian liturgical year that is known of by all and celebrated (albeit often perversely) by most. Popularly it may be considered to begin sometime in October with frenetic shopping in crowded shopping-malls, soon to be accompanied by ubiquitous trivial jingles and grotty grottos, and ending in the hangover of Boxing Day amidst mountains of discarded wrapping-paper, the boredom of children already weary of their new (and extraordinarily expensive) electronic toys, and the admission of over-indulgence together with the sadness (or perhaps relief) that it is all over for another year. One cannot help wondering how this over-commercialised, materialistic, consumerist, and indulgent celebration has anything whatsoever to do with the story of the birth of Jesus in an animal stall—and for many, of course, the celebrations have little or nothing to do with the event being celebrated though I want to suggest, later in this chapter, that such celebrations, perverse though they may be, may not be entirely unrelated or inappropriate. And for a surprising number in such an indulgent context the story of Christ's birth remains a central feature, albeit not an integrated feature, of the celebrations: school nativity plays persist and have not entirely succumbed to pluralistic political correctness; people do recognise the difference between 'Jingle Bells' and 'Once in Royal David's City'; and Midnight Mass remains one of the best attended Church services of the year.

---

[1] *CCP*, p. 91, and *The Promise of His Glory* (London: Church House Publishing and Mowbray, 1991).

There is something quite 'magical' about the atmosphere of Midnight Mass: an oasis of wonderment in the hassle of preparation and the round of office parties; a calm before the storm of turkey and presents; the comforting familiarity of a choir and carols; the gentle glow of candles and the repeating of half-forgotten liturgy; readings from Scripture that yet evoke memories of childhood and Christmases past; and the puzzling ritual of the Eucharist, the sheer oddity of encountering God (or being encountered by God) in bread and wine.

Whatever the Eucharist might be (or might not be) it isn't 'magic': there is no manipulation here, though there is expectancy; there is no incantation here, though there is prayer; there is no magic here, though there is mystery. The Latin term '*sacramentum*' came to be used to translate the Greek word '*musterion*' (μυστήριον) and though the Latin term had other, older references, this sense of mystery became central to the Church's understanding of the sacraments.[2] Within the history of the Church there have been several attempts to explain, or at least to interpret, this mystery together with some attempts to explain it away or to de-mystify it, but whether the Eucharist is interpreted as a transformation of substance, as a transformation of significance, as a transformation of identity, or as a spiritual dynamic without prejudice to the physical elements, the common underlying acknowledgment is that here we are dealing with a 'mystery', with something beyond the ordinary that defies explanation, with divine presence and action in and through but also beyond the physical elements of bread and wine. And what is true here is true of the sacraments generally: there is something happening here beyond the physical, beyond that which can commonly be observed and analysed; there is more to baptism than the dynamic of getting wet; there is more to marriage than a merely human covenant; there is more to ordination than the acknowledgment by the Church of a calling and of a ministry; etc. In each case we are dealing with mystery, with God's presence and action in and through but also beyond the merely physical; with a mediation of God's presence and action grounded in a promise and sought in prayer.

There is something especially poignant, then, in celebrating the Eucharist at midnight on Christmas Eve; of participating in that which is spiritual through the means of that which is physical in celebration of the second person of the eternal Trinity assuming our human, physical, flesh. There certainly is mystery here in the Christmas story, but there is more than mere mediation. Not even a high doctrine of transubstantiation as classically expounded by Thomas Aquinas affirms that the bread and

---

[2] An extended discussion of the sacraments will occur in chapter six of this book. For a full discussion of the sacraments and a theology of the sacraments see my earlier book, *Promise and Presence*.

wine of Holy Communion become the body and blood of Christ *while remaining bread and wine*. The doctrine of transubstantiation attests, on the contrary, that though the 'accidents' of bread and wine (their outward physical appearance) remain unchanged the 'substance' of bread and wine (which perhaps we could understand as their 'identity') is changed into that of the body and blood of Christ. But in the Incarnation of the Son of God there is no abolishing of physical human flesh nor is there any surrendering of the divine identity: the Word *becomes* flesh, and in that 'becoming' there is a miracle of even greater wonderment and a mystery of even greater depth. Here, alongside the doctrine of the Trinity, is the confession that renders Christian faith as uniquely Christian: that the Word of God, the eternal Son of the eternal Father, becomes truly human without ceasing to be truly God.

In the ancient world there were legends of the 'gods' taking physical form as men or women, as birds or animals, but these were no more than temporary appearances; there was no sense of an irrevocable 'becoming'. In some other religions, similarly, there are stories of 'gods' taking temporary physical form and even human beings who are revered as incarnations (or reincarnations) of a 'god', but the notion of the one God who is uniquely creator of all things becoming human, albeit in one of three eternal subsistences, is uniquely and distinctively Christian. The very idea of the Word becoming flesh, of God becoming human, of the Creator becoming a creature, of the divine becoming matter, was deeply incongruous if not offensive to those amongst whom the Christian gospel was first preached and it remains incongruous and offensive still. Indeed, the notion of God as the one who creates a material world out of nothing was deeply incongruous in the Greco-Roman world in which Paul preached and the Early Church grew. Spirit and matter were conceived as dualistically divided: God (or more usually some lesser 'god') may have shaped the universe out of already existing matter but no 'good' god could possibly create matter itself; matter is evil (or at least negative and limiting), only 'spirit' is good.[3]

In such a context, therefore, the Old Testament's affirmation of the material universe as God's creation and of the essential goodness of the material creation was radically distinctive. But even to most of those who affirmed the goodness of the material universe as God's creation (some of whom may have been more than a little influenced by the dualisms that were popular at the time) the proclamation of the Word's becoming flesh came as an offensive and blasphemous shock. God is God and creation is creation; the one is absolutely other to the other; the Creator

---

[3] Frances Young, '"Creatio ex Nihilo": A Context for the Emergence of the Christian Doctrine of Creation', *SJT* 44 (1991), pp. 139-51.

simply cannot become the creature. Well, who says so? As Karl Barth so sharply puts it,

> Who God is and what it is to be divine is something we have to learn where God has revealed Himself and His nature, the essence of the divine. And if He has revealed Himself in Jesus Christ as the God who does this, it is not for us to be wiser than He and to say that it is in contradiction with the divine essence.[4]

For the Christian Church it is the gospel story that is decisive and determinative for any understanding of God; God has defined himself in this story and any other notions of God, if they have any validity at all, must accord with this divine self-definition. It is the height of arrogance and folly to presume beforehand, on the basis of some other presumed knowledge of God gleaned from some other place, that which God truly is and that which God can or cannot truly do. Christian faith confesses the true God as truly defined in the gospel story: it is not merely that this baby born at Bethlehem is truly God; it is also and more fundamentally that God truly is as he is defined in this Christmas story which is at the same time the story recounted in Advent, Epiphany, Lent, Easter, Pentecost, and the celebration of his kingly reign. That God, in our human history, does this incomprehensible thing is defining of who God truly and eternally is; that he is the one who truly and eternally, but freely and graciously, is able to do this incomprehensible thing. We must remember, of course, that the story of Christmas does not define God simply and solely as the baby in the manger: the story of Christmas leads into the unfolding gospel story, celebrated in the Christian Year; it is the Son, the second person of the Trinity, and not the Father or the Spirit who takes flesh as Jesus of Nazareth; and this is something God freely and graciously does, it is not incongruous with his eternal nature and being but neither is it a necessity of his eternal nature and being. Yet for all these proper qualifications, Christian faith affirms that the true God is truly defined here, in the vulnerability of this infant life; in this radical coming that is, in fact, a becoming.

As was noted in the previous chapter, the non-necessity of this ultimate and definitive coming of God to his creation—which both retrospectively and prospectively is determinative of all his comings to his creation—is crucial if the distinction between God and the world, the Creator and his creation, is to be maintained. As was noted then, there are several contemporary and some more ancient theological constructions that tend to blur this distinction in order to stress the reality and profundity of God's immanence. But by so doing such attempts are often marked by attributing to creation itself that which Christian faith confesses uniquely of Christ: that God takes a body occurs uniquely here; it is Christ rather

---

[4] *CD* IV/1, p. 186.

than creation itself and as a whole who is the image of God; the eternal mutual indwelling (*perichoresis*) of the Father, the Son, and the Spirit does not extend to include creation; creation is granted its own contingent integrity. And as also was noted in the previous chapter, this blurring of the distinction between Creator and creation is generally a response to a more traditional Western tendency to define God's transcendent otherness in such a manner as to forfeit any meaningful notion of his immanence; creation is perceived as effectively independent, functioning mechanistically as a closed system with God banished to the margins of an original creative act. In radical distinction to both tendencies, and clarifying and specifying the confession of Advent, the Christmas story identifies the true God as the one who comes to his creation in this manner, in this particular, as this Jesus. He is not identified with his creation, he comes to his creation, but that he comes to his creation in this manner and in this particular signifies that he can do this, that this free coming is not incoherent or incongruent with his eternal being and nature.

In the light of this free coming of God to his creation, celebrated at Christmas, we have, then, to identify God's eternal being as open to the possibility of this event but not necessitating this event. This is a dangerously narrow tightrope on which to balance and proceed. God is simple. There can be no potentiality in God (since this would forfeit his simplicity). He comes as the one he is and was. This openness in God to come to his creation, then, must be essential to God's being in a manner that remains an openness rather than an inherent necessity (since any inherent necessity would forfeit God's transcendent freedom and render creation as necessary to God). The story of Christmas identifies the transcendent freedom of God as the positive, personal, and determinate freedom to do this amazing thing, to come to us in this becoming, rather than the arbitrary, impersonal, and indeterminate freedom to do this or not to do this. The freedom of God is the openness to this possibility, not the necessity of being the one who will do this, but the transcendent and free choice to be the one who can do this. On the basis of the Incarnation Karl Barth speaks of the eternal humanity of God and denies that there could ever be a 'manlessness' of God (*keine Menschenlosigkeit Gottes*).[5] The significance of this recurring and foundational theme in Barth is not a little disputed.[6] Barth is not simply eternalising the flesh of Christ since

---

    [5] Karl Barth, *The Humanity of God*, trans. John Newton Thomas and Thomas Wieser, Fontana Library of Theology and Philosophy (London and Glasgow: Collins, 1961). For a discussion of this theme (in German) see Eberhard Jüngel, '...*keine Menschenlosigkeit Gottes*... Zur Theologie Karl Barths zwischen Theismus und Atheismus', *Evangelische Theologie*, 31 (1971), pp. 376-90.
    [6] Kevin W. Hector, 'God's Triunity and Self-Determination: A Conversation with Karl Barth, Bruce McCormack and Paul Molnar', *IJST* 7.3 (2005), pp. 246-61; Bruce L.

that, once again, would be to render the Incarnation (and creation itself as its material context) as eternally necessary to God; the Incarnation occurs genuinely and uniquely in our human history as God's free and gracious act. But Barth is denying that the eternal Son is ever other than the one who assumes our humanity at Christmas; he is denying that God's freedom is ever other than the positive freedom to do this; he is denying that there is any Word of God other than the one who takes flesh here. There is never then, in this sense (for Barth), a *logos asarkos* (λόγος ἄσαρκος) but only ever a *logos ensarkos* (λόγος ἔνσαρκος).[7] I understand this (though I may be wrong) as an eternal openness to a possibility rather than an eternal actuality or even an eternal possibility, and it is this eternal openness in God's being, an openness inherent to his being, an openness to the possibility of the flesh assumed by the Son, and thereby an openness to the possibility of creation, that I here want to affirm and that the Church confesses as the significance of Christmas. Who God is here as the one who comes to us he ever was and ever is; the possibility of his coming to us in this radical manner is not a necessity of his eternal being and nature but neither is it a contradiction of his eternal being and nature; he is eternally open to this coming that is a reiteration of who he truly is. His freedom is the determinate freedom to do this and to be this. That God does this extraordinary thing in our human history signifies that he is able to do this and that this is inherent to his nature and not contrary to his nature. The simple freedom of God's eternal being is his freedom to be himself in this manner and not some foreign or arbitrary freedom; it is his freedom to be the one who comes to us in Christ.

Moreover, that God comes to us in this unique manner at Christmas is thoroughly definitive: it is definitive for who God is; it is definitive for who we are (a matter which will be discussed later in this chapter but which will be discussed more fully in chapter 4 of this book); and it is definitive for God's relatedness to creation. The prayers and responses recited at Christmas are traditionally a celebration of God as the creator in the context of a celebration of God as the one who comes to us in Christ. That the eternal Son becomes flesh at the Incarnation implies and presumes a created universe in which this historical event can occur (in this sense, as Karl Barth attests, creation is the context of the covenant).[8] But that the flesh assumed by the Son must imply an openness to this possibility in the nature of God more foundationally implies that this

---

McCormack, 'Karl Barth's Christology as a Resource for a Reformed Version of Kenoticism', *IJST* 8.3 (2006), pp. 243-51; Paul D. Molnar, 'The Trinity, Election and God's Ontological Freedom: A Response to Kevin W. Hector', *IJST* 8.3 (2006), pp. 294-306.

[7] *CD* IV/1, pp. 52-53.

[8] *CD* III/1, pp. 94-228.

gracious possibility of the Incarnation is simultaneously the ontological possibility of creation; that there is a material universe is a possibility rooted in the possibility of the flesh assumed by the eternal Son. Ontologically, though not temporally, the material flesh assumed by the Son is prior to the materiality of creation; the former is the ontological possibility of the latter (and in this sense, as Karl Barth similarly attests, the covenant is the context of creation).[9] The Word who becomes flesh is the one through whom and for whom all things were made.

The 'trappings' of the Christmas story, mobile stars and visions of angels, can blind us to the stark materiality of the story. There is nothing sentimental or twee about giving birth and passing a placenta, about the smell of animal stalls, about the messiness of nappies. And it is such sheer and stark materiality that God affirms so utterly at the Incarnation of the Son. It is not just the virgin's womb that he 'abhors not',[10] it is the entire materiality of creation in all its present messiness. He makes the flesh his own and thereby affirms it and fulfils it. And consequently, perhaps, the very materialistic manner in which we have come to celebrate Christmas may not be entirely misplaced. I am not, of course, implying that there can be any justification for commercial exploitation, for idolatrous greed, or for selfish indulgence. But the Bible (mercifully) says rather more about feasting than about fasting, and there is surely something appropriate in celebrating this divine affirmation of materiality with an affirmation of materiality rather than with an ascetic denial of materiality that implicitly repudiates doctrines of creation and Incarnation. That God is the creator of this material universe and has come so radically to this material universe can be celebrated appropriately in feasting, in the exchange of gifts, in the affections of human family life, and in acts of material generosity to the poor and the oppressed. The doctrines of creation and redemption are appropriately celebrated in a manner that does not implicitly deny their underlying affirmation.

On more than one occasion Colin Gunton praises the perception of Irenaeus, the second century bishop of Lyons, for the manner in which he relates and integrates an understanding of creation and an understanding of redemption. According to Gunton, this sharpness of perception has never quite been matched either in the Eastern or the Western traditions of the Church. Indeed, there is a recurring tendency in the Western tradition, notwithstanding the liturgy of Christmas, to separate and disconnect the two doctrines; whereas the liturgy of Christmas celebrates God's act of creation and God's coming to that creation in Christ in their togetherness and relatedness, most systematic treatments of the two

---

[9] *CD* III/1, pp. 228-329.

[10] 'O come, all ye faithful...' Latin 18th c. trans. Frederick Oakeley in *The Baptist Hymn Book* (London: Psalms and Hymns Trust, 1962), n. 104; cf. *Hymns Ancient and Modern* (London: Williams Clowes and Sons, 3rd edn, 1904), n. 59.

doctrines within the Western tradition tend to sever this connectedness and to treat them separately and distinctly.[11] While Augustine of Hippo (at risk of over-simplification) proposes that God creates a perfect universe, which falls from that original perfection through Adam's sin, and which is then restored to that original perfection through God's redemptive act in Christ, Irenaeus had previously assumed the original 'perfection' of creation to be a perfection with the potential for growth, development, and a coming to maturity and completion rather than a perfection of the already mature and complete—or, as Colin Gunton puts it, Irenaeus views creation as God's project, a project that only ever reaches its fulfilment in Christ.[12] During the Middle Ages and subsequently the Western tradition has occasionally pondered whether or not the Incarnation would have occurred had Adam not sinned and the related question of whether Adam sinned inevitably (though, of course, hypothetical questions in theology usually issue in confusion).[13] For Irenaeus (and for Colin Gunton) it is only in and through Christ that creation, and humanity within creation, reaches its goal and perfection; it reaches this goal in actuality in the context of Adam's sin and creation's fallenness, in the form of restoration as well as fulfilment; but the perfected humanity of Christ is ever the only means of the fulfilment of creation's perfection; creation comes to its goal here and not otherwise or elsewhere.

The celebration of God's act of creation as integral to a celebration of God's act of Incarnation is therefore a celebration of the purposefulness of creation and of the personal identity of that purposefulness. It is not only that the true God is truly identified in Christ; it is also that true humanity is truly identified in his real and risen humanity; and, in this real and risen humanity the goal and fulfilment of all creation is disclosed and effected. Christ himself is the source and purpose of creation. God's act of creation is therefore misunderstood and mis-celebrated unless it is understood and celebrated in this context and in this juxtaposition. This is our God, and this is who we are called and destined to be, and this is that which all creation is called and destined to be with us, and in and through him. Humanity and creation have no other valid goal than that which is revealed and effected here in Christ, in the Son's becoming flesh and in the perfecting of that flesh. The doctrine of creation, then, as comprehended in the light of the doctrine of the Incarnation, is not concerned merely with the zero point of time and space, nor is it concerned merely with the causal ground of the continuing existence of a

---

[11] Colin E. Gunton, *The Triune Creator: A Historical and Systematic Study* (Edinburgh: Edinburgh University Press, 1998).

[12] Colin E. Gunton, *Christ and Creation*, The Didsbury Lectures 1990 (Carlisle and Grand Rapids: Paternoster Press and Eerdmans, 1992); cf. Douglas Farrow, 'St. Irenaeus of Lyons: The Church and the World', *Pro Ecclesia* 4.3 (1995), pp. 333-55.

[13] For a brief discussion of this debate see Gunton, *The Triune Creator*, p. 121.

material universe, but rather and primarily a doctrine of creation thus comprehended asserts the reason for creation and for the continuing existence of a material universe; it identifies and declares creation's purposefulness and destiny. That there is a material creation, that moment by moment there is something and not nothing, is not just because there is a God who is the creator, the sole and sufficient cause of the universe, but because this, the true God, is Father, Son, and Spirit, is the one who comes in Christ to assume our flesh and to perfect it and to perfect us and thereby to perfect the universe. That there is a material creation is because this, the true God, invites and destines us together with all creation to participate in his glory in and through Christ and by the Spirit.

The true God, then, is not just the one who creates a material universe other than himself and continually dependent upon himself, he is also the one who destines that material universe to participate in his glory and to be a means of that glory. The new heaven and new earth that are to come are continuous and not discontinuous with this present heaven and earth. Redemption is the fulfilment, completion, and perfection of the material creation, not its abandonment and replacement. What is passing away is this material world's order (or disorder) rather than its materiality. Any vestige of gnostic dualism must be abandoned here: the material universe is created to be good and glorious.

The sacraments of the Church are of course, in part, affirmations and celebrations of this materiality. God who is freely other than the material universe and who has so radically come to this material universe in the becoming flesh of the Son, promises to mediate his presence and action, by the Spirit, through these material means. There is nothing inherent in the water of baptism or the bread and wine of communion, in the oil of anointing or in ministerial blessing, in the human love of a man and a woman, or the abilities of a Christian minister to render such as instrumental means of God's presence and action: that they become such is a matter of God's gracious promise; that they became such is a mediation of the Spirit; but that they become such is a further affirmation of the materiality of the created universe and of its purposefulness and destiny. God chooses these material means just as he chooses the flesh of Christ, just as he chooses men and women in Christ, just as he chooses creation itself.

And here as everywhere else and always the Spirit is the agent of this mediated presence and purposefulness. It is by the Spirit that we are re-created and transformed through the sacramental life of the Church; it is by the Spirit that Christ is born of the virgin Mary, by the Spirit that he ministers, by the Spirit that he offers his sacrifice, and by the Spirit that he is raised from the dead; and it is by the Spirit that the entire created universe is oriented to its goal and destiny in the Son. In granting creation its distinct and discrete existence God does not grant creation an independent and self-enclosed existence: creation exists contingently; it remains continually dependent upon the Creator; it has no other livingness than that sustained by the Spirit; moment by moment creation is God-breathed. This constant presence and action of the Spirit in creation is not empirically discernable: we hear the sound of the wind moving through the trees and we see the movement of the trees as the wind blows through them, but we do not hear or see the wind itself. And even were we to hear or to see the wind itself we would not hear or see the Spirit; we may hear and see the effects of the Spirit's presence and action within creation but, generally, we do not hear or see the Spirit, and that we perceive the effects of the Spirit's presence is a matter of faithful interpretation rather than mere observation. But perceived or unperceived, the Spirit who hovered over creation in the beginning continually moves through creation, breathing life into creation, and orienting creation to its true and only goal in Christ. The Christian doctrines of creation and providence should not therefore be too sharply distinguished: the triune God who brings creation into being is the one who sustains it in being and orientates it to this goal; creation is no less dependent upon God for its goal and its continuing existence than it was for its origin; in every sense the triune God is the 'cause' of the universe. Rightly understood there can be no Christian doctrine of creation without a doctrine of Christ and a doctrine of the Spirit: creation has this source, this goal, this manner of contingency, and this continuing divine presence.

To celebrate the coming of God to creation, therefore, is at the same time to celebrate that there is a creation to which he comes. To celebrate the Son's becoming flesh is to celebrate that there is material flesh for him to assume. Through the agency of the Son and the Spirit, the Father gives actuality to that which is other than himself; he not only brings a material universe into being, he maintains it and sustains it in being, in distinction from himself but also in continual dependence upon himself, and oriented to himself as the theatre of his glory. The eternal intimacy of the Father, the Son, and the Spirit, an intimacy disclosed in the gospel story, is reiterated in the unnecessitated but essentially coherent creative love of God for that which is other than himself, a love that brings that which is other than himself into existence, a love that sustains that which is other than himself in distinct but dependent existence, a love that freely invites and destines that which is other than himself to participate in his glory. The unnecessitated but essentially coherent love which issues in the Word becoming flesh is precisely the same unnecessitated but essentially coherent love which issues in creation and providence. God is love, and that love which is defined and interpreted in the gospel story is the love in which God creates the universe, sustains the universe, and orientates the universe to himself as its proper goal. And this love for that which is other than himself, which is a reiteration and echo of the eternal intimacy of

Father, Son, and Spirit, is the love in which he invites us to participate and the love he invites us to reflect and to mediate in the world.

Of all the virtues it is perhaps love that is the hardest for our contemporary society to comprehend and to define. In so many respects the English language is rich, with a range of terms conveying a range of nuanced significances, but the single word 'love' has so many meanings in so many different and diverse contexts. I can speak of the love that I have for God, the love that I have for my wife, the love that I have for my children, and the love that I have for my friends. Conversely, I can speak of the love that I have for good food, for country walks, for fast cars, or for comfortable shoes. I can speak of my love for my job and I can speak of my love for cricket. It is hard to think of another word in English that is so overused and so imprecise. And this overuse and imprecision is both unhelpful and confusing: my love for good food, for instance, is self-seeking and self-preserving (though not in any necessarily wrong sense); but all too easily I can import this self-seeking significance into my love for my friends, or even my love for my wife; all to easily that which should be self-giving becomes confused with that which is simply and solely self-serving and the morally good degenerates into the morally repugnant. Thomas Aquinas and the Latin tradition he exemplifies could ponder the distinction between *cupiditas* and *caritas*, the latter term conveying (as with its Greek counterpart) notions of grace, gratitude, and generosity, but while the English word 'charity' may have preserved this richness for William Shakespeare and for the editors of the translation of Scripture authorised by King James, to contemporary hearers the term merely denotes the giving of money or discarded clothes in aid of a good cause. But even the more ancient differentiation between cupidity and charity failed to distinguish the love that I have for my wife as self-giving and self-sacrificing rather than merely self-serving.

Few could have foreseen forty years ago how the relative reliability and availability of contraception would alter notions of public morality. Sever to such a degree the possibility and expectation of child birth from the act of sexual intercourse and the significance of the act of sexual intercourse is changed; the potentially procreational is re-envisaged as the merely recreational; the relationship expressed in sexual intimacy is no longer perceived necessarily as such a relationship as would be appropriate to the nurture of children. All this, of course, is not an inevitable outcome for all—the use of contraception need not imply that sex is reduced to the merely recreational, that a relationship has repudiated all openness to childbirth, that a relationship is of a nature and manner inappropriate to the nurture of children—but it seems to be an inevitable outcome for many: the manner in which sex is trivialised in the media is reflective of and programmatic for the manner in which sex is perceived in several sections of contemporary Western society. And in such a context the desire to give pleasure, to be for the other, is readily eclipsed by the desire to receive pleasure, to be merely for oneself. If the term 'love' is employed at all in such a context it is with a significance similar to a love for chocolate or fast cars. It is highly improbable that an act of intimacy so habitually formed by the desire for pleasure and the avoidance of enduring responsibility can be transformed simply through a wedding ceremony into an act of intimacy indicative of enduring responsibility and of a love that is unconditionally for the other. Old habits die hard. Here lies a major concern for the future of Western society, shaped so thoroughly by the trivialising stories promoted by the media. One cannot blame the development of effective contraception for the rise of abusive and self-serving sex (and all self-serving sex is abusive sex), human self-seeking is as long-standing as human existence, but this contemporary and popular trivialisation of sex to the merely recreational represents a more pressing and more foundational challenge to Christian virtue than related issues of cohabitation, divorce, and re-marriage.

It is with the societal consequences of this trivialisation of sex that we should be most concerned since, in such a context, misapprehensions of the significance of love are compounded. A love that is merely self-gratifying can hardly be the sum of the virtues and a love that is no more than sexual attraction will prove insufficient to sustain the nurture of families. There is nothing inherently wrong with the chemical reaction that is romantic love—we are made this way—but that which may begin with sexual attraction must grow and deepen into an unconditional being for the other if a relationship is to be sustained and is to be capable of sustaining others.

The love which the triune God invites us to share, to reflect, and to mediate is the love which is his triune nature, the love defined and interpreted in the gospel story, the love that freely issues in creation and redemption, the love that is rightly identified as the sum of the virtues. All that is faithful, hopeful, temperate, just, wise, and enduring is included here and ultimately defined here. This is the single and perfect nature of God and this is the nature into which he will perfect his creation. In all eternity the intimacy of Father, Son, and Sprit is mutually affirming, mutually consenting, mutually inter-penetrating. So absolute and absorbing is this triune love that were it not truly triune, were it not mediated through the person of the Spirit, the love between the Father and the Son would draw them to collapse into an indistinguishable monad.[14] And this mutual love of Father, Son, and Spirit is reiterated in God's unnecessitated love for his creation in Christ. That God freely

---

[14] For a discussion of this understanding of the trinitarian relationships, and of my indebtedness to Tom Smail for the development of the idea during one of many happy conversations, see my *Promise and Presence*, pp. 38-41; cf. p. 39, fn. 65.

loves and redeems that which is other than himself, that God freely creates that which is other than himself, is a gratuitous overflowing of the true God's triune intimacy. There is nothing self-serving in this divine love: in love God invites us to participate in his glory but his glory is neither enhanced nor diminished by our participation. His love for that which is other than himself is a reiteration of his perfect love within himself and not an addition to it. Even the assuming of flesh by the Son is a reiteration of this triune love and not an addition to it or an amendment of it. God is perfectly loving in himself without us; his love for us is an entirely gratuitous openness to that which is other than himself.

Love so defined, then, love that is this perfect mutual intimacy, love that freely takes our flesh and in that flesh freely embraces crucifixion, love that gratuitously gives existence to that which is other and sustains that dependent but distinct existence of the other, this is the love we are invited to share, to reflect, and to mediate. This love is properly defined as 'charity' (*caritas*): it is gratuitous, it is generous; it is identified as a disposition that issues in acts rather than as the acts themselves; it is a gratuitous and unconditional being for the other.

In the Hebrew Old Testament there is one recurring term that seems to signify the single and undivided nature of Israel's God: it is the word '*chesed*' (חסד), a word variously translated into English as 'steadfast love', 'loyalty', 'faithfulness', 'covenant love', 'loving-kindness', 'mercy', though it is quite impossible to convey in any single English word all the nuances of meaning that seem to accrue in Israel's history and scriptures to this single Hebrew word. This single Hebrew word comes to convey who God has demonstrated himself to be faithfully and unchangingly in his covenant relationship with his people. The group of words translated as 'holy' or 'holiness' (קדוש; קדש), of course, may have a rival claim to a summarising conception of God's single nature—and certainly in Reformed systematic theology, if not elsewhere, a notion of God's holiness came to predominate—but in the Old Testament (if not also the New) the notion of holiness seems to be principally negative, conveying the sense of God's separateness from his creation and from human sinfulness (and thereby, positively, conveying a notion of God's aseity, his self-sufficiency). The word '*chesed*' (חסד), by contrast, identifies who this self-sufficient and separated God is, both in relation to his people and in himself; it identifies his nature positively rather than merely negatively; and its significance is to be traced through the unfolding narrative of God's story with his people rather than by the excavation of any more general root 'meaning' for the word. God's covenant love for his people is entirely a matter of grace: it is free and gratuitous, but it is also utterly faithful and constant; it is never merited by God's people and, though it certainly has consequences, it is wholly unconditional. God never promises to be the God of Abraham or the God of Israel 'if...'; he rather promises to be the God of Abraham and the God of Israel 'therefore...'. The commands given to Israel through Moses are the consequences of the covenant rather than the conditions of the covenant: it is because God has redeemed Israel as his people that he calls them to live by these distinctives. Should Israel fail to live by these distinctives God will not cease to be Israel's God, he will not repudiate his covenant, he cannot deny his essential nature, but he will be Israel's God in purifying judgement which is the form his unchanging covenant love takes when it is opposed or rejected.[15]

And when in Micah's prophecy God's dispute with his people is dramatically narrated, when God asks his people how he may have wronged them, when God declares through the prophet that he has no need of their offerings or of 'rivers of oil', he reminds them that what he does require is that they 'act justly', 'love mercy', and 'walk humbly' with him (Micah 6.8). The middle requirement here translates this same Hebrew word '*chesed*' (חֶסֶד): this which is positively the essential nature of God, his merciful love, his covenant faithfulness, is what he desires to characterise his people; he seeks that same merciful love and covenant faithfulness in them as is defining of him. In Hosea too (which along with Jeremiah is probably the most sustained and graphic exposition of God's covenant faithfulness to his people, a merciful love that accompanies them into the judgement of the exile in order to woo them again to himself) it is this same covenant love that God desires from his people and in his people:

> ...I desire mercy, not sacrifice,
> And acknowledgment of God rather than burnt offerings. (Hosea 6.6)

This verse from Hosea is twice cited by Jesus within the narrative of Matthew's Gospel, firstly in response to the Pharisees when Jesus is criticised for mixing with tax collectors and sinners at Matthew's party (Matthew 9.13), and secondly, again in response to the Pharisees, when Jesus' disciples are criticised for plucking ears of corn on the Sabbath (Matthew 12.7). The Pharisees at the time of Jesus were the spiritual heirs of the Hasidim of the Maccabean period (the word 'Hasidim' derives from the Hebrew word '*chesed*' [חֶסֶד]), these were the ones who remained faithful to the covenant through ruthless persecution and oppression, yet it was precisely this virtue of merciful, faithful love that Jesus found so lacking in the Pharisees. That which God seeks from us is not arid legalism or sacrifice but that faithful and merciful love which is the reflection and mediation of his own essential nature. And it is this covenant love, this essential nature of the one true God, that takes our

---

[15] *CD* IV/1, pp. 40-41; cf. pp. 220-24.

flesh at Christmas. Here, and here alone, in the humanity assumed by the second person of the Trinity, the eternal covenant love of God is answered and mediated in humanity. The gospel story is the ultimate narration of God's essential nature in our humanity, its depth and its consequences. The gospel story, then, is the ultimate command or invitation of God to humanity, that we should be such a people, shaped in this manner.

The love that is ultimately defined in the gospel story, the love that is narrated throughout the Old Testament, the love that issues both in creation and redemption, the love that is the essential nature of the true God who is Father, Son, and Spirit, is that which is freely, faithfully, and unconditionally for the other. It is grace and it is marked by uncalculating generosity. And, thus defined as that which most profoundly expresses the essential nature of God, it is the sum of the virtues; it is not set over against holiness, justice, mercy, righteousness; it is inclusive and defining of such.

It is love so defined, rather than mere sexual attraction or self-serving desire, that is the essence of marriage: a love that implies consequences but which is unconditional (for better or for worse, for richer or for poorer, in sickness and in health); a love that is faithful and seeks faithfulness; a love that is generous rather than grasping; a love that is both trusting and merciful; a love that seeks to serve rather than to be served; a love that is freely for the other and that, through sexual intimacy, is welcoming of children.

But it is the Church, rather than marriage, that is called to be the principal and most profound reflection and mediation of the faithful and merciful love that is God's eternal nature; it is the Church that is the deeper 'mystery' or sacrament (Ephesians 5.21ff.). Perhaps it was for this reason that Jesus became so impatient with the Pharisees: their pettiness was a denial of their true calling. Certainly it was this covenant faithfulness that God sought with so little effect from Israel. And one cannot help but conclude that he continues to seek it with little effect in the Church. Our divisions, our rivalries, our disloyalties, our lack of mercy, all are denials of the Church's calling and essence. It is still true that God desires mercy rather than sacrifices or legalism.

With reasonable consistency the Christian tradition, at least since Augustine, has defined sin as that which militates against love.[16] Christ calls us to love God with our whole being and to love our neighbour as ourselves, and it is that which militates against this love, displaces or

---

[16] See for instance Aurelius Augustine, *On Christian Doctrine*, trans. J.F. Shaw, in *NPNF*1, vol. 2, pp. 513-97, I 22-40; *ST* I-II 71-74; *Institutes* II 8; John Wesley, *A Plain Account of Christian Perfection as believed and taught by the Reverend Mr. John Wesley, from the year 1725, to the year 1777* in *The Works of the Rev. John Wesley*, vol. XI (London: Wesleyan Conference Office, 1872), pp. 366-446.

distorts this love, which is the root and essence of sin. Martin Luther, in expounding the Ten Commandments, similarly identifies idolatry as the root of sin since it is false or misdirected love.[17] All acts of selfishness, envy, greed, faithlessness, cruelty, violence, unkindness, all are manifestations of disoriented or perverted love. I may have faults or habits which give offence (although none is intended) but which in no sense militate against my love for God or my neighbour—such is venal sin. But every disposition, word, or act that in any manner militates against love for God and love for neighbour is mortal sin, is a repudiation of God's covenant with men and women that is the true deity and humanity of Jesus Christ. And of such mortal sin I am unequivocally guilty, and so are you, and so are we all. In response to the unequivocal love of God narrated to us in the gospel story, both as the love in which he embraces us and the responsive love he invites from us and that is enfleshed in the perfected humanity of Jesus, we can only confess ourselves as sinful and as sinners, as those who have not loved God with our whole being, as those who have not truly and faithfully loved our neighbours. We can only throw ourselves again on the fathomless mercy of God. We can only pray again, as so many times before, that through our worshipful indwelling of the gospel story at Christmas, and throughout the Christian seasons, we will be shaped by that story more and more to be those whose lives are wholly for God and wholly for one another.

> Almighty God,
> who called your Church to witness
> that you were in Christ reconciling the world to yourself:
> help us so to proclaim the good news of your love
> that all who hear it may be reconciled to you;
> through him who died for us and rose again
> and reigns with you and the Holy Spirit,
> one God, now and for ever.
> Amen.[18]

---

[17] For a discussion of this see Stanley Hauerwas, 'The Truth about God: The Decalogue as Condition for Truthful Speech' in *Sanctify Them in the Truth*, 37-59.

[18] *CCP*, p. 103, and *ASB*.

CHAPTER 3

The One Who Is Revealed

> Lord our God,
> who anointed your only Son
> with the Spirit at the river Jordan,
> and so hallowed the waters of new birth
> to bring us forth to salvation:
> keep us strong in the life of grace,
> direct the ways of your people,
> and open the door of your Kingdom
> to all who stand upon the threshold of faith;
> through Jesus our Messiah and Saviour…
> Amen.[1]

In 1998 Neil MacGregor, then Director of the National Gallery, delivered the F.D. Maurice Lectures at King's College, London, on the theme of 'seeing salvation'. This series of highly engaging and perceptive lectures would issue in a major exhibition at the National Gallery, a popular television series, and a splendid book.[2] He began his lectures by considering a painting that was an interpretation of the presentation of the infant Jesus at the Temple in Jerusalem and on the words Luke records as spoken by Simeon that would provide the title and focus for the entire series:

> Sovereign Lord, as you have promised,
> you now dismiss your servant in peace.
> For my eyes have seen your salvation,
> which you have prepared in the sight of all people,
> a light for revelation to the Gentiles
> and for glory to your people Israel. (Luke 2.29-32)

Here again we encounter the incomprehensible claim that stands at the heart of Christian faith, that God's salvation can now be seen, that God

---

[1] *CCP*, p. 114, and Ven. David Silk, *Prayers for Use at the Alternative Services* (London: Mowbray, 1980).

[2] Neil MacGregor and Erika Langmuir, *Seeing Salvation: Images of Christ in Art* (New Haven, CT: Yale University Press, 2000).

himself has taken physical, visible form amongst us in the person of the Son, that we have seen his glory. As Neil MacGregor reminded us, it was the confession that God had made himself visible in Christ that was to prove decisive in the 'iconoclast' controversy of the eighth century: to prohibit images now would be implicitly to deny this historical making visible that is the essence of the Christian gospel. Nowhere is this visibility and tangibility more starkly expressed that at the beginning of the first Epistle of John:

> That which was from the beginning, which we have heard, which we have seen with our eyes, which we have looked at and our hands have touched—this we proclaim concerning the Word of life. The life appeared; we have seen it and testify to it, and we proclaim to you the eternal life, which was with the Father and has appeared to us. We proclaim to you what we have seen and heard, so that you also may have fellowship with us. And our fellowship is with the Father and with his Son, Jesus Christ. We write this to make our joy complete. (1 John 1.1-4)

The gospel story is precisely this: it is a story. It is not a collection of esoteric philosophical musings, nor is it a reflection upon a series of mystical experiences or contemplative insights. The gospel story is a narrative, or rather a series of narratives; it issues from the testimony of those who saw and heard and touched; it is witness to that which became visible and tangible in our human history. And, as Simeon prophesies, this salvation is made visible not just to Israel, as the historic people of God, but also to the nations. The confession of Christ as the light for the nations is one possible reading of the emphasis of Matthew's Gospel: the four women included in the genealogy with which the Gospel begins may be included simply because they are women, may be included because they are initiators who move Israel's story forward in significant though differing ways,[3] but they may also be included because they were non-Israelites; it is not Jewish shepherds who come to worship the infant Jesus in Matthew's birth-narrative but enigmatic 'Magi', representatives of a foreign and pagan religion; and the Gospel concludes with the ascending Christ claiming all authority in heaven and on earth and consequently commissioning his followers to make disciples of all nations. But this conclusion of the Gospel is interesting not just for its universal commissioning; it is interesting also for the surprising aside that, even in the presence of the risen Christ, there were some disciples who saw, heard, and touched, but who still 'doubted' (Matthew 28.17). The Magi relate their revelation to Herod, but in Herod it evokes a rather different response.

---

[3] I am grateful to Anne Elizabeth Clements, one of my postgraduate students, for drawing my attention to this possibility.

When in the prologue to John's Gospel the writer confesses that 'we have seen his glory' the 'we' is not all inclusive. The scribes and Pharisees saw the same Jesus, heard the same teaching, witnessed the same miracles, but with a very different outcome. When Lazarus is brought back from the dead there are many who come to believe in Jesus, but there are others who report the miracle to the Sanhedrin who, in turn, conclude that Lazarus as well as Jesus must now be killed. There were others in the Temple courts on the day that the infant Jesus was presented who certainly did not recognise what was recognised by Simeon and Anna.

The liturgical season of Epiphany is a little ambiguous, having rather different significance and rather different focus in the Eastern tradition than in the Western tradition. The focal narrative for the Western tradition at Epiphany is the presentation of Christ to the Magi as significant of Christ as the light of the world, the light to the nations. Within the Eastern tradition, Epiphany tends to be granted greater emphasis and significance than Christmas and, as the name of the season implies, there is similar celebration of Christ as the light to the nations, of the making visible of God's saving presence in Christ, but here the focal narrative is the story of Jesus' baptism, of the declaration of his sonship, of this making public of his identity. As a consequence, within the Eastern tradition (and increasingly now in the Western tradition), alongside a focus on this making visible of God's presence in Christ there is also some focus on baptism itself and prayer for those who 'stand upon the threshold of faith'.

We will reflect in the next chapter on the significance of Jesus' baptism for Jesus himself, a significance that can be inferred particularly from the telling of the story by Mark and Luke, a significance that is explicitly tested in the story of Jesus' wilderness temptations that immediately follows the story of his baptism in the Synoptic Gospels. In Matthew's Gospel, however, we are perhaps intended to infer that the declaration 'This is my Son, whom I love; with him I am well pleased' (Matthew 3.17) is directed to John the Baptist, to the gathered crowd, and to us as readers of this testimony. And John's Gospel is explicit that the descending Spirit is seen by John the Baptist as confirmation that this is the one 'who will baptise with the Holy Spirit' (John 1.32-33), that this is 'the Lamb of God, who takes away the sin of the world' (1.29), that this is 'the Son of God' (1.34). What John the Baptist is enabled to see, therefore, is proclaimed to all but not necessarily heard and believed by all or perceived and recognised by all. Jesus is present in the river Jordan for all to see, but do all really hear the Father's owning of the Son, and do all really recognise the Holy Spirit coming upon him in anointing? The 'epiphany' which is the baptism of Jesus is a trinitarian dynamic; the Son here is only disclosed as the Son through a declaration by the Father and a descending by the Spirit. Epiphany, therefore, cannot be reduced to a supposed objective givenness; God's light does not shine here (or anywhere else) in such a manner as to be visible to independent and detached human reason. When Simon Peter, at Caesarea Philippi, confesses Jesus as the 'Christ, the Son of the living God', Jesus doesn't congratulate him on being bright enough to work this out for himself, he rather tells him that this has been revealed to him by the Father (Matthew 16.16-17). Jesus is never truly known merely humanly or in detachment: 'No one knows the Son except the Father, and no one knows the Father except the Son and those to whom the Son chooses to reveal him' (Matthew 11.27). Here, at least, perception is a spiritual dynamic, a trinitarian dynamic. But perhaps more generally there is more to hearing than an uttered sound; there is more to perceiving than an object to be seen.

In what is intended as no more than a sketch of dogmatics there clearly isn't space for an extended and sufficient discussion of notions of perception. Philosophy throughout the centuries has pondered this dynamic without ever coming close to an agreed conclusion. At one extreme of the debate (at risk of some over-simplification) is the notion that objects somehow communicate their properties to our perception. At the other extreme of the debate (and again at risk of some over-simplification) is the notion that perception is all that there is, that there is no objective reality corresponding to our perception. For the sake of being really confusing, there are 'hard' and 'soft' versions of 'realism' and there are 'hard' and 'soft' versions of 'anti-realism' or 'non-realism'. But quite distinct from all 'self-contained' attempts to account for perception, there are theological accounts of perception which, albeit in differing ways, understand perception as a gift: it isn't that the object is simply available and accessible to my perception; nor is it that my perception is itself creative of the object; it is rather that God, who alone by his perception is creator and sustainer of all that really exists, grants to me perceptions of discrete reality (or perhaps better, grants to me to share in his own perception of discrete reality). In a quite excellent (and commendably brief) discussion of revelation Colin Gunton comments that we need a general theology of revelation before we can come to a theology of general revelation and that the former identifies all knowledge, and not just our knowledge of God, as a gift.[4] Jonathan Edwards, the eighteenth-century philosopher and Reformed theologian, argues that all perception is a participation through the Spirit in God's creative perception and that, therefore, human sin issues from an active

---

[4] Colin E. Gunton, *A Brief Theology of Revelation* (Edinburgh: T & T Clark, 1995), pp. 20-39.

distorting of the manner in which we have been given to perceive.[5] That I perceive anything at all is a gift; an active 'being-givenness' rather than an objective 'givenness'. That I perceive anything at all other than in the manner in which it is being given to me by God to perceive is perversity.

To perceive Jesus at all, as the baby in the manger, as the carpenter's son from Nazareth, is itself a gift, an active and mediated 'being-givenness'. To perceive Jesus as the 'Christ', as the Saviour of the world, as the eternal Son become flesh, is similarly a gift, a mediated 'being-givenness'. But if the latter is the manner in which God the Father perceives Jesus of Nazareth, and if any perception we have of Jesus (or of anything or anyone else) is a participation by the Spirit in the Father's perception of Jesus, then any perception of Jesus that falls short of the Father's perception of Jesus is a distorted perception, it is unfaithful, untruthful, sinful.

And if this is true of our seeing it must also be true of our hearing and reading; what is true of perception must also, by inclusion rather than extension, be true of communication. Given the difficulties of human language identified previously, it is surprising that communication ever occurs: my words are insufficient to my concepts and those same words may signify rather different concepts to my hearers; the relationship between words and ideas or things, between signs and that which is signified, is largely arbitrary; significance is therefore a matter of convention; communication can only ever occur in communities; I need not only to be able to speak your language, I also need to inhabit your community, I need, at least to some degree, to share your language conventions. And where your words are written rather than spoken, read rather than heard, the problem is further compounded; I have that much less chance of grasping the significance of your words; I am that much more removed from your immediate community; you, as the writer of those words, are removed to me, are effectively 'dead' to me.

But what if communication, like perception, is not just a human and 'given' dynamic; what if communication, like perception, is acknowledged as a spiritual and 'being-given' dynamic; what if the living God actively enables human communication in resonance of his eternally perfect triune community? This world may be God-forsaking but it is never God-forsaken. The Spirit through whose living agency the world was formed in the first instance continues to be present in and through all creation, giving life and breath to all that is living, *and enabling perception and communication amongst all that is living*. Since the Spirit was the means of the effectiveness of God's initial creative word, might

---

[5] Jonathan Edwards, *Notes on the Mind*, in *YE* 6, *Scientific and Philosophical Writings*, ed. Wallace E. Anderson (New Haven, CT, and London: Yale University Press, 1980), pp. 339 and 364; cf. Colwell, *Living the Christian Story*, pp. 36-38.

not the Spirit also be the means of the effectiveness of all words, of all communication? This is a radical proposal (and I don't expect it to be widely welcomed) but I believe it to be both radically consistent and persuasive. The Western tradition has not been short of attempts to moderate divine causality, to maintain creation's discrete integrity by banishing God to the margins of an initial creative act and (increasingly rare) 'miraculous interventions'. A radically theological account of all reality should not be beguiled by such immanence denying tendencies: divine causality, in every sense and in every respect, is the basis rather than the denial of human and creaturely causality. To acknowledge creaturely perception and creaturely communication as continually dependent upon divine causality is radically consistent rather than innovative; it is following Colin Gunton in proposing a general theology of revelation as the basis of a possible theology of general revelation.

And this general theology of revelation (or better in this specific, a general theology of communication) is, of course, the basis for a theology of general revelation, or rather, of revelation generally (traditional Protestant distinctions between 'general' revelation and 'special' or 'particular' revelation, as Karl Barth notes, are usually unhelpful and confusing—if revelation, properly speaking, is God's self-disclosure, revelation of God's self rather than mere information about God, then there can never be anything 'general' about such self-disclosure).[6] Christian preaching, like any other form of human communication, is a spiritual dynamic: that ideas and information are communicated by a preacher to a congregation is mediated by the Spirit; it is a gift; there is here as always in all human communication a spiritual dynamic of 'being-givenness'. But Christian preaching properly understood is more than the mere communication of ideas and information, more even than the effective and transformative communication of ideas and information; Christian preaching is transformative rather than merely informative specifically because it occurs in response to a command and promise of God and it is ventured in humble expectation of the fulfilment of that promise; it is a mediation by the Spirit of God's own transforming presence. Through the mediating agency of the Spirit the gospel message is not just heard (though it would not even be heard without such mediating agency), it is indwelt, and it is indwelt in such a manner that issues in living encounter, and this living encounter issues in change. As with all that is truly sacramental this dynamic of transforming presence cannot be presumed upon, it is promised but it cannot be manipulated, it can only be sought and anticipated in prayer. But it is on the basis of this command and

---

[6] *CD* II/1, pp. 257-321; cf. Wolfhart Pannenberg, *Systematic Theology*, vol. 1, trans. Geoffrey Bromiley (Grand Rapids, MI: Eerdmans, 1991), pp. 95-118.

promise, and in conscious dependence upon the Spirit's mediating agency, that Christian preaching properly takes place.[7]

The phenomenon of Christian preaching is clearly a dynamic, an event, something takes place. A hearer may refuse to listen but a hearer has no power to manipulate the words of a preacher, they are not at the hearer's disposal. For the greater part of the Church and for the greater part of the Church's history the same has been the case with Holy Scripture: Scripture has been read and heard in a liturgical context, as integral to an act of worship, and with consequent sacramental expectation of the Spirit's mediation and transforming presence. For the greater part of the Church's history a significant number of Christians have been unable to read, they could 'only' listen. But more significantly, for a greater part of the Church's history the Scriptures were otherwise unavailable to the greater number of Christians—printing had not yet been invented; copies of the Scriptures were not yet readily available. And as I have bemoaned elsewhere, there is nothing like having a copy of the Bible at your disposal for encouraging the mistaken assumption that the Bible is at your disposal.[8] The apparent 'object' nature of books as paper and ink within cardboard or leather binding beguiles us into the false assumption that texts are objects at our disposal, that there is a 'givenness' here rather than a 'being-givenness', that the dynamic of writing and reading has an objectivity lacking to the dynamic of speaking and hearing, that this is not a 'dynamic' at all but a 'static'. But as has already been noted in this discussion, and as the rise of post-structuralism and deconstructionism illustrates, precisely the opposite is the case: the dynamic of writing and reading—and it is a dynamic—is more problematic than the dynamic of speaking and hearing; the author is removed as is the author's immediate community of communication; the appearance of 'givenness' is delusory. Inevitably, therefore, the act of reading any text is creative of significance; fresh nuances and inferences can be drawn with every fresh reading; no amount of historical excavation can unearth an author's intended meaning with final certainty; only the trace of an author's intention lingers.[9] And what may be less immediately apparent but which is no less inevitable is that the act of reading any text is similarly and simultaneously creative of a reader: a reader is drawn into a text and is changed by a text;[10] a reader is rendered by a text just as a text is

---

[7] Karl Barth, *Prayer and Preaching* (London: SCM Press, 1964).

[8] Colwell, *Promise and Presence*, ch. 4.

[9] Jacques Derrida, *Of Grammatology*, trans. Gayatri Chakravorty Spivak (Baltimore: John Hopkins Press, 1974), pp. 62ff.

[10] See for instance Paul Ricoeur, *Hermeneutics and the Human Sciences: Essays on Language, Action and Interpretation*, ed. John B. Thompson (Cambridge: Cambridge University Press, 1981), pp. 101-28, esp. p. 112.

rendered by a reader; or, to put the matter another way, texts are dangerous.

Christian theology should not be unduly disturbed by this apparent collapse into unqualified subjectivity (which, as Stanley Fish points out, is not, and could not be, a collapse into unqualified subjectivity in any case[11]); a radically theological account of all reality—the confession that there can be no creaturely causality that is not rooted, enabled, and encompassed by divine causality—acknowledges a spiritual mediation of all human communication, written or spoken; a radical Christian theology rejoices, therefore, in the 'being-givenness' of texts and in the 'being-formedness' of readers. That texts are rendered by readers and that readers are rendered by texts is a spiritual, and not merely a human, dynamic. In a God-breathed world there is no human communication, written or spoken, that is not mediated by the Spirit. The 'being-givenness' of Scripture, then, in one sense, is no different from the 'being-givenness' of any and every text; in and through any and every act of reading the Spirit mediates significance to us and we are being shaped by that mediated significance.

But, unlike other texts, the 'being-givenness' of Scripture comes to us with sacramental promise: Scripture is read as 'Scripture' with the promised expectation of a mediated and transforming encounter with the true and living God of whom Scripture witnesses. This inspiredness of Scripture in the event of reading is without prejudice to the inspiredness of Scripture in the event of its writing—that probably unconscious mediation by the Spirit in and through the human authors of Scripture whereby their genuinely human words became and become the means of God's word without ceasing in any respect to being genuinely human words—that it is the faith of the Church that the Holy Spirit gave Scripture as Scripture through the means of human authors and their human words is not here in question. But this original 'being-givenness' of Scripture is similarly without prejudice to its present 'being-givenness' in the event of reading or hearing, nor does the former render the latter redundant or superfluous. Scripture is not the Spirit's prison; the mediated Word of God is not here simply 'given' in a manner that renders it at our disposal, accessible to our detached observation, vulnerable to our manipulation. Despite common appearances and assumptions to the contrary, no text is ever simply available to us in this detached, static, and objective manner. And Scripture as 'Scripture' could not possibly be available to us in such a manner: Scripture can only be read as 'Scripture' in response to a sacramental promise of the Spirit's

---

[11] Stanley Fish, *Is There a Text in This Class? The Authority of Interpretive Communities* (Cambridge, MA, and London: Harvard University Press, 1980), pp. 317-21.

mediating presence and action; Scripture can only be read as 'Scripture' in prayerful expectation for the fulfilment of this promised mediated presence, an expectation that is humbly confident but never arrogantly presumptuous. The true and living God is never simply at our disposal, in creation, in the event of the Incarnation, in Christian preaching, in Scripture, in the Church, in the sacraments, or anywhere else.

Through the mediating agency of the Spirit the living God grants us to read Scripture as the means of his promised transforming presence, he grants us to hear Christian preaching similarly, and through these mediating means he grants us to perceive the living Jesus as the one he truly is. And since this is the manner in which God gives us to read, to hear, to see, to perceive, to perceive other than in this 'faithful' manner is an active distortion of this 'being-given' perception, it is perversity, it is 'faithless', it is sinful:

> ...even if our gospel is veiled, it is veiled to those who are perishing. The god of this age has blinded the minds of unbelievers, so that they cannot see the light of the gospel of the glory of Christ, who is the image of God. (2 Corinthians 4.3-4)

With the word 'faith' we have the opposite problem to that which we encountered with the word 'love'. Whereas the single English word 'love' now serves to convey so many diverse nuances of significance, nuances of significance that were conveyed by a range of words in Greek, in Latin, and even in older forms of English, in contemporary English we have a range of possibilities for translating the single Greek word 'faith' ($\pi\iota\sigma\tau\iota\varsigma$); possibilities that convey very different nuances of significance. This single Greek word '*pistis*' ($\pi\iota\sigma\tau\iota\varsigma$), so prominent in the New Testament, is variously rendered by the English words 'faith', 'belief', 'trust', 'loyalty', 'confidence', 'faithfulness', 'trustfulness', or even occasionally 'commitment'. Just as there can never be a non-interpretative reading of any text there certainly can never be a non-interpretative translation of any text: translators come to texts with their own defining stories and presuppositions; they may themselves be interpreted by the texts they translate but they interpret those texts in that process. Choices have to be made and are made inevitably not just with respect to the world of the text but also with respect to the world of the translator. Any claim to an exact or precise translation wholly misapprehends the nature of language, the dynamics of writing and reading, of speaking and hearing. This dynamic of ultimate imprecision and inevitably interpretative translation is only problematic when it is not acknowledged and admitted. Here, as everywhere else, we are doing the best we can, but that 'best' is irresolvably our own; we are who we are with the previous stories and prejudices that we bring to the task of translating. As with any other service within the Church, the work of the translator should be humbly offered rather than presumptuously imposed. The best I can ever do is to offer a translation as my own reading of the text, a reading (I hope) that is careful and informed, but a reading that inevitably is my own, albeit in my connectedness to the reading community which is the Church catholic. And when translators are confronted by this Greek word *'pistis'* (πίστις) this dynamic of interpretative translation, of bringing suppositions to a text at the same time as being shaped by a text, is at least as prominent as anywhere else.

The matter is perhaps best illustrated by recent trends in reading Paul's Letter to the Romans. Following Martin Luther's cataclysmic change of understanding and direction, Protestant theology (and, to a degree, Catholic theology in response to Protestant theology) has become accustomed to reading the Epistle as a treatise on the means of salvation: we are 'justified' (declared to be 'righteous' in a legal sense) through our 'faith' (in the sense of 'believing' the gospel) rather than through the 'works' of the 'Law' (in the sense of any effort on our part to earn our salvation), and this has occurred through divine election (in the sense of God choosing us in distinction to others), an election illustrated by his previous choice of Israel. The most glaring difficulty of this interpretative strategy is that it reduces chapters 9 to 11 as a mere illustration of the closing verses of chapter 8 and leaves the final five chapters of the Epistle as a series of discrete ethical instructions, unrelated to the preceding argument. But what if chapter 12 and following identify the reason for the Epistle? And what if we recognise that the climax of Paul's argument occurs at the doxology which concludes chapter 11 rather than the declaration of assurance which concludes chapter 8?

There are new perspectives on Romans rather than a single and agreed new perspective (though there are common themes and insights shared, to a significant extent, by a series of commentators) and it would be beyond the scope of this work to engage in this debate in any sustained manner beyond the identification of a series of possibilities.[12] The first possibility, already intimated, is that chapters 12 through to 16 identify the reason for the Letter and its preceding argument; that Paul's concern is not primarily with the means of salvation but rather with the need for Jewish and Gentile Christians to accept one another within a single and undivided Church. Consistent with this possibility and the recognition that

---

[12] Krister Stendahl, *Paul Among Jews and Gentiles* (Philadelphia, PA: Fortress Press, 1976); E.P. Sanders, *Paul and Palestinian Judaism: A Comparison of Patterns of Religion* (Minneapolis, MN: Fortress Press, 1985), *Jesus and Judaism* (London: SCM Press, 1985), and *Paul, the Law and the Jewish People* (London: SCM Press, 1985); J.D.G. Dunn, 'The New Perspective on Paul', *Bulletin of the John Rylands Library* 65 (1983), pp. 95-122, *Jesus, Paul and the Law: Studies in Mark and Galatians* (London: SPCK, 1990), *The Theology of Paul's Letter to the Galatians* (Cambridge: Cambridge University Press, 1993); with Alan M. Suggate, *The Justice of God: A Fresh Look at the Old Doctrine of Justification by Faith* (Carlisle: Paternoster Press, 1993).

Paul's argument reaches its climax in the doxology that concludes chapter 11 is the possibility that God chooses Israel, and now chooses the Church, not over against the rest of humanity, but in order that finally he might 'have mercy on them all' (11.32). It is surely more likely that references to 'Law' ($\nu \acute{o}\mu o\varsigma$) relate to Israel's covenant law (*Torah*), which functioned (and functions) in a very different manner to Roman law (*lex*), and that therefore a notion of forensic justification (equivalent to acquittal in a criminal court) is unlikely to be the significance of Paul's use of the term 'righteousness' ($\delta\iota\kappa\alpha\iota o\sigma\acute{u}\nu\eta$). There is then the further possibility that Paul's primary concern is to declare God's righteousness, a righteousness personified in Christ, and God's own faithfulness to his covenant (a faithfulness confirmed rather than denied through the salvation of Gentiles), to which the active faithfulness of Christ is a response (a faithfulness anticipated and typified in Abraham).[13] And if the latter is the case then it is surely more likely that, in response to this active righteousness of God, we are made righteous by the Spirit through Christ (rather than merely declared righteous), and that in response to this active faithfulness of God we are called to faithfulness, a faithfulness demonstrated and fulfilled in Christ and which was always the true goal and demand of Israel's covenant law.

In summary, and for the limited purposes of this chapter, it is possible (and more coherent) to understand 'righteousness' ($\delta\iota\kappa\alpha\iota o\sigma\acute{u}\nu\eta$) in Romans as being made righteous, rather than merely being declared righteous ('justified'), as an echo and outcome of the righteousness of God in Christ; and similarly it is possible (and more coherent) to understand 'faith' ($\pi\acute{\iota}\sigma\tau\iota\varsigma$) in Romans as covenant faithfulness in echo of and in response to God's covenant faithfulness and the faithfulness of Christ. The systematic and formulaic distinction between 'justification' and 'sanctification' so characteristic of Reformed debates ought not to be read back into the New Testament where the two terms seem to be used almost interchangeably and without such marked distinction. And, other than in the ridicule of the notion in the Epistle of James, I doubt that the word 'faith' ($\pi\acute{\iota}\sigma\tau\iota\varsigma$) is ever used within the New Testament with the significance of mere 'belief'. Yet mere belief is, I suspect, the common contemporary connotation of 'faith', a connotation reinforced by recitation of the Christian creeds without noting their proper context in worship and Christian commitment.

This is not to deny that an element of 'believing that' is basic to any notion of faith and faithfulness: '…anyone who comes to [God] must believe that he exists and that he rewards those who earnestly seek him'

---

[13] I remain grateful to my colleague David Southall for drawing my attention to these possibilities, both through his continuing research and in his earlier work: David Southall, 'The meaning of $\delta\iota\kappa\alpha\iota o\sigma\acute{u}\nu\eta\ \theta\epsilon o\hat{u}$ in Paul's Epistle to the Romans' (Spurgeon's College, the University of Wales; unpublished MTh dissertation, 2002).

(Hebrews 11.6). But even here it may not be quite sufficient to interpret belief as the mere acknowledgment that something is the case, that God exists and that his nature is such as to do this. Surely one should infer an active trust here beyond a mere acknowledgement that something is the case? In the examples of faith recorded in this chapter of the Letter to the Hebrews we are reminded of those who trusted God and who lived on the basis of God's promises. This is more than merely believing that something is the case; it is a trustful confidence that this is the case, it is a faithful coherence of living.

The radically theological account of perception outlined previously confirms faith as a form of knowing, a form of knowing that is consistent with the manner in which God gives us to know, a being awakened to participate in his triune perception. This 'being-given' perception can, of course, be resisted, refused, and rejected. I can refuse to perceive as God perceives, to affirm as God affirms, to love as God loves; I can refuse to know by faith; I can know without faith and against faith. But such knowledge is distorted; it is a rejection of God's light; it is a knowledge still bounded by darkness:

> ...light has come into the world, but people loved darkness instead of light because their deeds were evil. All those who do evil hate the light, and will not come into the light for fear that their deeds will be exposed. But those who live by the truth come into the light, so that it may be seen plainly that what they have done has been done through God. (John 3.19-21)

The basis of faith as a form of knowing is simply to know in this manner; it is to participate in a mediated perception; it is to see light in God's light (Psalm 36.9). But faith as this embracing of mediated perception cannot remain as mere perception; to know in such a manner is to be shaped and changed by that knowledge. Because Simeon had seen God's salvation he could depart in peace; because the Magi saw a star in the East they came to worship; because John the Baptist saw a dove and heard a voice he proclaimed Jesus as the one who would baptise in the Spirit; because Saul of Tarsus saw a vision on the Damascus road he became Paul the apostle. A significant aspect of Jonathan Edwards' contribution to thought was a rejection of any separation of knowledge and affection: to know is to be affected by that knowledge; no knowledge leaves us unaffected.[14] And the principal affection evoked by a knowledge of God as rendered in the gospel story is trust, or better 'trustfulness'. Faith is not merely a knowledge of God mediated by the Spirit, it is a trustful resting in this God as prompted by the Spirit. Epiphany is a celebration of a light that has shone and is shining—it shone in Christ, and it shone into our lives—and as a celebration, Epiphany is a response of gratitude and of

---

[14] Jonathan Edwards, *Religious Affections*, in *YE*, 2, ed. John E. Smith, pp. 93-99.

trust, we have seen this light and we have confidence in this truth; we have come from darkness to light. To have come to see this light which shines through the gospel story, to have come to see it without refusing it, rejecting it, or perverting it, is to live trustfully. In and through the gospel story God has reconciled us to himself, he has demonstrated that he is for us and not against us, that nothing can separate us from his love, that this is who he is and ever shall be. In and through the gospel story God has confirmed his trustworthiness and it would be sheer perversity, therefore, not to trust him, not to live trustfully. There is, of course, much that might militate against such trust: the universe is not yet as God ultimately wills it to be; we ourselves are not yet as God ultimately wills us to be; there is yet much that appears to conflict with God's ultimate will as revealed in the gospel; there is yet much that we do not understand. But we have been brought to see all reality in the light of this light, to trust even through darkness and confusion. Our trust is not that all will turn out alright in the immediate or even the penultimate future; our trust is not in God *for* anything; our trust is in God himself; our trust is therefore in God *through* everything. The trustfulness that is evoked in us in response to the mediated light of the gospel is not an impersonal expectation for penultimate health, wealth, or happiness; it is a personal confidence in the one who can be trusted ultimately and therefore can be trusted through all that is penultimate.

But that faith which is the evoked response to the mediated perception of God's light is more than confident trust, is more than assurance. All perception to some degree is transforming and therefore perception of the divine is divinely transforming. In the gospel story God has demonstrated his absolute and eternal faithfulness: the gospel story is the fulfilment of his covenant with Abraham and with Israel and not its denial or repudiation; God is utterly constant; he cannot change; he cannot deny himself. To perceive this faithfulness of God in the gospel story, then, is to be shaped in faithfulness; we are invited through the gospel not just to believe, not just to trust, but to live coherently with this belief and this trust; to live truthfully; to live faithfully. Just as God is utterly faithful as the one he is, utterly loyal to his covenant, utterly constant, so we are invited to reflect his faithfulness, his truthfulness, his constancy; we are being shaped though our indwelling of the story as faithful people, truthful people, constant people.

There is much in our present context of post-modernity, of course, that militates against faithfulness. We are caricatured (and we caricature ourselves) as a generation of 'non-joiners', as those who shy away from permanent commitment. Our generation is marred by the tragedies of soaring divorce rates and abortion rates—both to a significant degree (albeit very differently) being indicative of relationships that fall short of faithfulness. There may be many reasons prompting cohabiting couples to delay or to reject the formal commitment of marriage, but one reason in at least some (if not the majority) of instances is a reluctance to exchange vows of life-long fidelity—and surely this reluctance is more honest than the exchanging of such vows while reserving some unspoken qualification of those vows: not a commitment 'for better or for worse' but a commitment 'just as long as this seems to work out okay'. And it is not just in personal relationships but also in commerce, industry, and business life that there appears to be a breakdown of trust—penalty clauses in contracts are indicative of such anticipated breakdown. Moreover, in health care and education the ubiquity of evaluation exercises (with little acknowledgement that, in both spheres, that which is most significant cannot be so readily quantified) similarly signifies a breakdown of trust.

Through the gospel story we are invited to faithfulness not just in relation to God but also in relation to one another, in our sexual relationships, in our friendships, in our business relationships, in our serving, our caring, and our mentoring. To lack faithfulness in any context is to live untruthfully, to live in a manner inconsistent and incoherent with the gospel story. Truly to perceive this light is to be changed by this light thoroughly and utterly. To believe in this salvation and this Saviour is to be transformed in faithfulness in reflection and echo of his faithfulness. The Church is called to witness to this truth, to this light that has shone in our lives, to this which we have been brought to perceive. To witness to this is certainly to speak of this and to speak truthfully of this, but to witness to this is also to live truthfully, coherently, faithfully and to do so in every context and in every relationship. I cannot speak of this light truthfully while living untruthfully. I cannot be faithful to God while being unfaithful to my wife, to my friends, to my colleagues, to those with whom I do business, to those whom I serve in any way.

The virtue which is faithfulness, like love and hope, is a gift of the Spirit. Like every virtue it is a habit but it is not a habit that can be acquired through merely human effort and practice. It is given by the Spirit in response to the perception of the light of the gospel, indeed, it is integral to that perception. But, as with love and hope, this gift of faithfulness is mediated by the Spirit, not in abstraction, but through the particular habits which are the sacramental life and worship of the Church. It is as we indwell the gospel story through our indwelling of the Church, through our hearing of preaching, through our hearing and reading of Scripture, through our participation in the sacraments, and through our participation in one another, that we are shaped in faith and in faithfulness. The season of Epiphany is a celebration of the shining of God's light, through the gospel story, to Israel and to the nations. And it is as we indwell this gospel story through our celebration of Epiphany and the liturgical seasons that we are brought by the Spirit to perceive this light and to reflect it, to believe and to live faithfully.

> Almighty God,
> from whom all thoughts of truth and peace proceed:
> kindle, we pray, in every heart, the true love of peace
> and guide with your pure and peaceable wisdom
> those who take counsel for the nations of the earth;
> that in tranquillity your Kingdom may go forward
> till the earth is filled with the knowledge of your love;
> through Jesus Christ our Lord…
> Amen.[15]

---

[15] *CCP*, p. 126.

CHAPTER 4

The One Who Journeys To The Cross

Almighty and everlasting God,
you hate nothing that you have made
and forgive the sins of all those who are penitent:
create and make in us new and contrite hearts
that we, worthily lamenting our sins
and acknowledging our wretchedness,
may receive from you, the God of all mercy,
perfect remission and forgiveness;
through Jesus Christ our Lord...
Amen.[1]

In Matthew's account of the baptism of Jesus, as noted in the previous chapter, the voice from heaven seems to be directed to us, to the crowd standing nearby, to John the Baptist. The accounts of Jesus' baptism narrated in Mark's Gospel and Luke's Gospel, however, seem to imply a rather different significance. Instead of the words 'this is my Son...' (οὗτός ἐστιν ὁ υἱός μου) we find the words 'you are my Son...' (σὺ εἶ ὁ υἱός μου), the identification is addressed to Jesus himself and only secondarily, perhaps, to others who might hear or read—which raises the unanswerable but nonetheless interesting question of Jesus' awareness of his own identity. It is foolish and inappropriate to try to construct a Christology by speculating concerning the self-consciousness of Jesus: we are not given to know this; self-consciousness is a contemporary concern rather than (apparently) a concern at all for the authors of the New Testament; and a doctrine of Christ's identity as truly human and truly divine must be established on more stable and substantial grounds than psychological speculation. But the question is intriguing, and there is much in Luke's narrative, in particular, that serves to encourage such speculation. Elizabeth speaks of the unborn child in her womb leaping with joy at Mary's greeting (Luke 1.44), but this may be hyperbole and it would be presumptuous to infer from this a degree of consciousness, self-consciousness, and recognition in yet unborn infants. Indeed it would be incoherent to assume that the zygote forming in Mary's womb, a

[1] *CCP*, p. 140, and *ASB*.

fertilised egg, a collection of dividing cells, would or could be 'conscious' in any meaningful sense. Did the baby in the manger know his true identity as the eternal Son of the eternal Father? Some sentimental carols and Christmas cards seem to imply such but such would be extraordinarily problematic and the Gospels' narratives imply no such thing. On the contrary, Luke comments (more than once) that the child Jesus 'grew', not just in 'stature' but also in 'wisdom' and in 'grace'. John Owen (1616–83), the Puritan divine, opines that '[t]he human nature of Christ was capable of having *new objects* proposed to its mind and understanding, whereof before it had a *simple nescience*'.[2] Jesus learnt things—there is no reason to assume otherwise—and, in consequence, it is entirely reasonable to assume a growing awareness of his identity and mission. Luke narrates a story of the boy Jesus in the Temple knowing that he needed to be in his 'Father's house' (2.49), but then Luke repeats the observation that Jesus 'grew' and records, at his baptism, a heavenly voice confirming his identity. Moreover, the first question in Jesus' wilderness temptations, both in Luke's account and Matthew's account, challenges this identity: '[i]f you are the Son of God...'

The habit of speculating concerning God's nature in abstraction from the gospel story issues in the assumption that perfections of God's freedom—omnipotence, omnipresence, omniscience, etc.—are essential to God's nature in an abstract and indeterminate sense. But what if, in the light of the gospel story, we recognise God's freedom as determinate rather than indeterminate: his omnipotence as the freedom to assume our weakness in the person of the Son; his omnipresence as the freedom to be present in this particular and in this manner; his omniscience as the freedom to know in the Son in the manner that we know? What if, therefore, we acknowledge the true freedom of the true God to be the specific freedom of his love to do this astonishing thing in assuming our human flesh in the person of the Son? I am not suggesting for a moment that this resolves the mystery of Christ's identity as truly God and truly human, but I am suggesting that allowing divinity to be defined in the gospel story, rather than in abstraction, eases the difficulty of affirming that Jesus is *really* human while remaining truly divine.[3] The affirmation of Christ's real humanity need only be at the expense of his true divinity if divinity is defined other than in the light of the gospel story. The affirmation of Christ's divinity, when that divinity is defined as it is

---

[2] John Owen, *A Discourse concerning the Holy Spirit* (1674), in *The Works of John Owen*, vol. 3, ed. W.H. Goold (London: Banner of Truth, 1965), p. 170.

[3] Karl Barth, amongst others, makes use of the distinction between Christ's 'real' humanity (as we are really human) and Christ's 'true' humanity (as we are less than truly human other than in him) and I will exploit this distinction in this and in the next chapter. *CD* III/2, pp. 132-202.

defined in this particular, is not at the expense of the reality and particularity of his humanity.

The doctrine that the single person of Christ participates fully in two natures, the divine and the human, that he is of one substance with the Father according to his deity and of one substance with us according to his humanity, but that this union of natures is without confusion or change or division or separation, that the distinctive characteristics of these two natures are preserved and concur in this one undivided person—this is the faith of the Church confessed at the Council of Chalcedon (451), but it is easier to confess than to comprehend. The heated debates leading up to the Council, and in its immediate aftermath, and ever since; questions of whether Christ's single person implies a single will, or whether his two natures imply two wills; questions of whether it is Christ's single person that participates fully in the properties of both natures or whether the properties of each nature are communicated to the other; questions of whether Christ's miracles are manifestations of his divine nature or rather manifestations of the Spirit working through his human nature—all such questions demonstrate the extraordinary difficulty of maintaining each element of the confession of Chalcedon without prejudice to every other element of the confession. Such difficulty ought not to surprise us: we are reflecting here on an event that is unique, without parallel, and without analogy; we shouldn't expect such reflection to be easy, but we should persist in the effort. The essence of Christian faith is at stake here. Without this confession we have nothing to say. The Church's faith is nothing but the faith that both deity and humanity are defined in the one who is rendered in the gospel story. There is no other ultimately valid definition of deity and humanity. Christ is not a hybrid, not a confusion or mingling of deity and humanity; he is fully God and fully human. God is truly defined in this single person and our humanity similarly is truly defined here. Christ is not human at the expense of being God and neither is he God at the expense of being human.

And it is the reality and particularity of Christ's humanity, and in consequence the reality and particularity of our humanity, that focuses our prayers, our reflections, and our spiritual disciplines during the season of Lent. Whatever Jesus may or may not have known of his divine identity, and at whatever stage he may have known such, there never was and there never would be any question whatsoever concerning the reality of his humanity—at least for him and for those immediately around him. His conception was miraculous but his birth was as our birth with all the dependency and vulnerability of pregnancy and infancy, with all the messiness of birth and after-birth. He would have dirtied his nappy, just as any other baby, and there is no reason to suppose that his childhood and puberty were not precisely as ours. The Epistle to the Hebrews speaks of him being 'made like his brothers and sisters in every way' (Hebrews 2.17) and there can be no good reason to doubt or to qualify this summary. The canonical Gospels tell us little of Jesus' childhood and nothing of this youth, and there is no reason to suppose that there was anything here other than the ordinary: a first-century Jewish man living within the confines of his own particular context. His perfection (or sinlessness) had everything to do with his growing sense of identity, his relationship to the Father (a relationship here, as in eternity, mediated by the Spirit), and his increasing awareness of his mission. But his perfection (or sinlessness), I suspect, did not mitigate in any respect the normal dynamics of growing up, the tensions of family life, or the struggles of adolescence.

And so he arrives at the river Jordan to be baptised by John; and so he comes to hear this voice from heaven, attesting his identity; and so he receives an anointing of the Spirit, separating him to his unique mission; and so he journeys into the wilderness, to fast and to pray. Like us he is tired. Like us he is hungry. Like us he is weak. And like us he is tempted. He is tempted to satisfy his hunger. He is tempted to the spectacular and to put his relationship with the Father to the test. He is tempted to seek power and authority by doing obeisance to that which is unworthy. He was 'tempted in every way, just as we are…' (Hebrews 4.15).

Now I may be unusual but I have never been tempted to turn stones to bread, no-one has ever offered me universal power, and I have never thought of throwing myself from a high building. (I'm scared of heights.) Conversely, Jesus was never tempted to travel on a bus without paying his fare, he was never tempted to cheat on his wife, he was never tempted to distort a claim for expenses, he was never tempted to break a speed-limit or to park illegally. There are innumerable temptations common to contemporary society that Jesus would not have known. There are temptations that would have been as common in his society as today but which were not particular to him. When the Letter to the Hebrews speaks of him being 'tempted…as we are' we should not infer that every temptation known to us or known to any man or woman throughout history was similarly and with identical force known to him—that would be silly. We should rather infer that, though his temptations were particular to him (just as all our temptations, in actuality, are particular to us as particular men and women), the dynamic of temptation was for him as it is for us. There are some temptations which I do not find remotely tempting, possibilities which others find alluring but which leave me entirely unaffected. Similarly there are some things that have always been alluring to me that would prove unproblematic for many others. I'm only tempted by what is tempting to me, by what I find desirable and alluring though ultimately dishonouring and destructive. That which is not in some way desirable is not tempting in any meaningful sense. Consequently, if Jesus was really tempted, that is to say, if his being tempted was not a meaningless charade, there was that which was actually tempting to him, that which for him was desirable and alluring. He was hungry, and to abuse his authority to turn stone to bread was genuinely tempting. He was vulnerable to the allure of universal authority through illegitimate means. He was susceptible to the possibility of the dramatic. And, very much more profoundly, in each of these instances he was tempted by the possibility of proving his identity, to others if not to himself. In all this he was genuinely tempted but in no respect did he give way to this temptation. The desire was real but the desire was immediately and absolutely rejected. He was 'tempted in every way, just as we are — yet was without sin' (Hebrews 4.15).

Whatever is intended by affirmations of the sinlessness of Jesus such must be without prejudice to the genuineness of his temptation, the reality of his humanity, the depth of his vulnerability, the radical degree of his dependence upon the Spirit. At this point some elements within the Christian tradition have faltered, affirming the essential sinlessness of Jesus as the one who is truly God at the expense of the genuinely dynamic sinlessness of Jesus as the one who is really human, the actuality of his temptation and of his overcoming of that temptation. Jesus is true to himself but he is freely true to himself. He is not an automaton. His being tempted is not a charade. He truly comes to the place, context, and humanity that is ours but, in that humanity, he is true to himself, he does other than we have done, he resists temptation, he honours his Father, he lives by the Spirit. On occasions within the Christian tradition the question has focused on whether the Son assumes a 'fallen' or 'unfallen' humanity,[4] but this distinction is not entirely helpful: to state the obvious, 'unfallen' Adam 'fell'; he was capable of sinning; he was capable of giving way to temptation. More particularly, notions of the 'fall' itself, together with related notions of original righteousness, original sin, original guilt, and the nature of justice all require distinct and careful definition, definition, that is, that begins with the Christ narrated in the gospel story and focuses here, rather than definition which begins somewhere else — with the story of Adam, for instance — and attempts to fit Christ into a predefined schema. These are issues to which, albeit in a limited way, this chapter will return. But the two affirmations that must be made at this point, and throughout every discussion of Christ's person, are that he truly comes to the place which is ours but that, in that place, there is never a shadow between him and the Father.

---

[4] For the most famous (or infamous) discussion of this see Edward Irving, *Christ's Holiness in Flesh, The Form, Fountain Head, and Assurance to us of Holiness in Flesh* (Edinburgh: John Lindsay, 1831).

Maybe it is in Gethsemane rather than in the wilderness that the particularity of Christ's temptation—its focus, its depth, its dynamic—is disclosed. There is no hint of charade here: he is in agony, his sweat is like drops of blood. As is entirely understandable, he shrinks from the prospect of the Cross; the longing that this cup should be removed from him is genuine and profound. There is a reality of desire here and there is therefore a reality of temptation. But Christ does not give way to this desire; he does not turn away from his Father's will; he commits himself to that will, albeit with genuine dread. In this narrative of Christ's praying in Gethsemane—a narrative that identifies his mission and that thereby summarises his life to this point, and a narrative that so graphically anticipates his suffering and death—the dynamic significance of Christ's perfection is identified. The perfection of Christ is not primarily a matter of his sinlessness, a matter of that which he ought not to do and does not do; it is primarily a matter of his obedience, a matter of what he ought to do and does do. The Letter to the Hebrews (again) speaks of Christ having 'learned obedience' through suffering (Hebrews 5.8), he was *made* 'perfect through suffering' (2.10). The perfection of Jesus is not a static of his identity but a dynamic of his living obedience; it is his resolute commitment to the goal that is his mission; as he came to understand that goal, there was never a point at which he turned from that goal or from a manner of living appropriate to that goal. Jesus Christ ever is who he is; he is 'the same yesterday and today and for ever' (13.8); but who he is, and the manner in which he is who he is, is established in the narrative of this story of his mission, of his temptation, of his suffering, and of his death.

And that which perfection is for Christ it is derivatively also for us. Sin is not primarily our doing that which ought not to be done (though such is the inevitable consequence of that which is sin primarily); sin primarily is our failure to do that which ought to be done, our failure to love God utterly and to love one another in reflection of that love for God. In Christ and empowered by the Spirit we are invited to participate in this loving obedience: to fulfil this goal is perfection; to fail to fulfil this is sin. And, apart from Christ, we have not fulfilled this.

The story of Gethsemane is significant for the definition of the reality of Christ's temptation, but more basically it is significant for the definition of his humanity and, thereby, for the disclosure of our humanity in the gravity of its predicament. The humanity disclosed at Gethsemane is humanity in agony, humanity called to drink of this cup, humanity facing suffering and death, humanity in the place of judgement. In Matthew's account of Jesus' baptism we find a reluctant John: 'I need to be baptised by you, and do you come to me?' (Matthew 3.14). John was calling men and women to a 'baptism of repentance for the forgiveness of sins' (Luke 3.3), but Jesus was without sin, he had nothing of which to repent, he had no need of forgiveness; John recognised him as the coming Messiah through whom forgiveness could be received and through whom the Spirit would be given. So why was Jesus baptised and how might his baptism 'fulfil all righteousness' (Matthew 3.15)? Beyond Jesus' somewhat enigmatic reply, this question is never explicitly answered in the Gospels, but maybe we should understand Christ's baptism, like Gethsemane, as anticipating (and thereby interpreting) his Cross. He comes to the river Jordan and, though himself without sin, he identifies himself wholly with repenting sinners. Though without any need for forgiveness, he invites his disciples to join him in his praying by saying 'our Father...forgive us our debts...' He comes to Gethsemane and, though this cup is ours and not his, and though he shrinks from drinking it, he accepts it as his Father's will and as the fulfilment of his mission. He is brought to the place of human judgement and, though he is guilty of no crime, he is condemned and Barabbas walks free. He is led to Golgotha and nailed to a Cross and, though this accursed place could never justly be his, he dies there for us and for our sin. The humanity assumed by the eternal Son is our humanity, not just in its temporal and spatial locatedness, its limitedness, its weakness, its vulnerability, its dependency, its exposure to temptation, but also in its sinfulness, its suffering, its death, its existence under curse and under judgement.

Jesus knew no sin but he was made sin for us (2 Corinthians 5.21). The stark shock and seemingly contradictory assertion of this text has led some to interpret the second occurrence of the word 'sin' ($\dot{\alpha}\mu\alpha\rho\tau\dot{\iota}\alpha\nu$) in this verse as 'sin offering'.[5] Certainly there are instances where the Greek word seems to bear this latter significance, but surely it is unlikely that the word would be employed with such different meaning within a single sentence and, even more decisively, that which more simply is asserted here is asserted again and again (though perhaps less starkly) throughout Scripture—that Christ comes to take our place:

> ...he was pierced for our transgressions,
> he was crushed for our iniquities;
> the punishment that brought us peace was upon him,
> and by his wounds we are healed.
> We all, like sheep, have gone astray,
> each of us has turned to our own way;
> and the LORD has laid on him the iniquity of us all. (Isaiah 53.5-6)

Whatever (and whoever) the prophet may originally have envisaged, the New Testament, and consequently the Church, interpreted this (and

---

[5] See for instance the margin reference in *NIV*.

similar passages) in the light of Christ and, thereby, interpreted Christ in the light of this (and similar passages). Though we ought not to read later notions of retributive penalty back into such texts (contrary to common tendencies in both Catholic and Protestant theology) what is plainly (and unanimously) asserted is that Christ comes to take our place, a place that was ours and not his, but a place that he has made his own. Further discussion of 'models' of atonement will be postponed until the next chapter: all that needs to be noted at this point is the antiquity and ubiquity of this notion of a 'glorious exchange'. Famously Gustav Aulén identifies the notion of victory as the classic understanding of the atonement predominant in the Early Church,[6] but it could be argued that this notion of a 'glorious exchange' is as long established and was more commonplace. Athanasius, for instance, speaks of the work of Christ as overcoming corruption and death,[7] but he does so in the context of the underlying notion of a glorious exchange—he takes our flesh that we might share his glory; he dies our death that we might share his resurrection; he becomes human that we might become divine.[8] And though the New Testament certainly attests Christ's victory over sin and death, and though its predominant imagery for Christ's death is that of sacrifice, the recognition that Christ has come to take our place, albeit variously expressed, is repeatedly stated. He is the one who gives his life as a 'ransom for many' (Matthew 20.28); he is the one who is given that we might have eternal life (John 3.16); he is the one who, though rich, became poor so that we through his poverty might become rich (2 Corinthians 8.9); he is the one 'who loved me and gave himself for me' (Galatians 2.20); he is the one who died 'so that by the grace of God he might taste death for everyone' (Hebrews 2.9). The place that the eternal Son of God takes at the Incarnation, at his baptism, and at the Cross, is our place rather than his, and he takes it that it might be our place no longer but that we might share in his place which is the true destiny of our humanity,

Rather, then, than arguing over whether or not Christ assumes 'fallen' human nature (having defined the fall and fallenness in some other place and by some other means) we need to acknowledge that our fallenness is finally defined here (rather than somewhere else), in the flesh assumed by the Son and in the outcome of that assumption. It is our place, and not merely the appearance of our place, to which he comes, and in coming to

---

[6] Gustav Aulén, *Christus Victor: An Historical Study of the Three Main Types of the Idea of the Atonement*, trans. A.G. Herbert (London: SPCK, 1931).

[7] Athanasius, *On the Incarnation*, trans. A Religious (London: Mowbray, 1953), II 8 and 9.

[8] Athanasius, *On the Incarnation*, VIII 54: Αὐτὸς γὰρ ἐνηνθρώπησεν, ἵνα ἡμεῖς θεοποιηθῶμεν. The significance of this most radical expression will be considered in the next chapter.

it he defines it. Unless he comes precisely to our place he cannot bring us to his place. He assumes our humanity and in the act of that assumption he exposes the reality of our humanity for what it presently is, in its sinfulness and corruption:

In that He takes our place it is decided what our place is.[9]

There may never have been a clearer expression of this idea than that which occurs in Karl Barth's discussion of Jesus Christ as 'The Judge Judged in Our Place'.[10] In the first place, Christ comes as the judge, displacing us from a place we have usurped but, at the same time, relieving us of an onerous burden.[11] But without ceasing to be the judge, he also takes our place as the judged; without himself sinning he takes responsibility for our sin and our being as sinners and thereby relieves us of that responsibility; our being as sinners is no longer a matter that is in our hands since he has taken it into his hands.[12] Thirdly, and decisively, he is actually judged in our place, not merely taking our place in this judgement but, by doing so, making an end of sin and of us as sinners.[13] And finally, he acts justly in our place to establish that which is just; to establish and to reiterate God's eternal 'Yes' to humanity.[14] In all this there is no thought of any disjunction between the Father and the Son; no thought of the Father exacting vengeance on the Son instead of exacting vengeance on us. The thought is rather of the Son taking the place of us as sinners, displacing us from that place, and in that place which is ours making an end of sin and of us as sinners; exposing our sinful state and identity in the very act of dealing with it and with us. And in all this he is not only the judge but the judged: he is the judge in the act of being judged and he is judged in the act of judging, he establishes justice through the judgement he brings and the judgement he endures.

In the 'Paradise' story of Genesis 2.4–3.24 we have the account of Adam's sin and expulsion from the garden together with Eve but, arguably, we do not encounter a 'doctrine' of the Fall, or of 'original sin', until Paul's exposition of the matter in Romans 5.12ff. (stated more briefly in 1 Corinthians 15.22) where our identity in Adam is acknowledged in the light of our identity in Christ. At very least we should recognise that our identity in Christ is noetically (as a matter of knowledge) prior to our identity in Adam. But surely this is insufficient: there cannot be two rival and distinct definitions of humanity (in Adam

---

[9] *CD* IV/1, p. 240.

[10] *CD* IV/1. pp. 211-83.

[11] *CD* IV/1, pp. 231ff.

[12] *CD* IV/1, pp. 235ff.

[13] *CD* IV/1, pp. 244ff.

[14] *CD* IV/1, pp. 256ff.

and in Christ); rather humanity is authentically, primarily, and ultimately defined in Christ while only inauthentically, secondarily, and penultimately defined in Adam. Our identity in Christ is ontologically as well as noetically prior to our identity in Adam; it is a priority of being as much as a priority of knowing. There is, therefore, no definition of 'true' humanity as chosen by God (of 'original righteousness') other than in Christ (a matter that will be explored more fully in the next chapter). But neither can there be an ultimate definition of 'untrue', inauthentic, sinful humanity other than in Christ, in his passion, in his Cross, in the judgement he assumes and absorbs in our place. The story of the Fall and of 'original sin' is the story of Adam, but the ultimate definition of the Fall and of 'original sin' is the story of Jesus, of his Cross, of the place he takes on our behalf. Ultimately it is only here that we are brought to recognise the dire gravity of our sinfulness, of our rejecting of God, and its eternally fatal consequences; to repeat Barth's maxim: '[i]n that He takes our place it is decided what our place is'.[15]

Contrary to Augustine and to so much of the Western Christian tradition, I am no more defined by Adam's sin through being his genetic descendent than I am defined by Christ's righteousness through being his genetic descendent. It is rather that the story of Adam's sin, albeit in a secondary and provisional manner, is defining and descriptive of my life and of the lives of every man and woman. We, like Adam, have wilfully done that which we ought not to have done by wilfully not doing that which we ought to have done, by wilfully refusing to trust God and to live within the bounds set for us. But it is in the story of Christ and his Cross that our being in sin in all its desperate hopelessness and lostness is decisively defined and described. In the impenetrable darkness of the crucifixion and in Jesus' cry of forsakenness he takes our place of lostness and abandonment in a separation from God which, by us rather than him, has been wilfully chosen and embraced. There is no element of this lostness and abandonment that he does not fully enter and fully feel. He makes this place his own though it is not his own; but in making this place his own he renders it ours no longer. This inauthentic place which we have chosen and which he has taken is no longer authentically our place. He and he alone is rejected in this place of sinfulness and judgement in order to bar this place of rejection to us eternally. What it means to be in Adam is decisively disclosed in the story of Jesus rather than the story of Adam. What it means to be the sinner in abandonment, rejection, and judgement is revealed at Calvary rather than in Eden.

The story of Jesus is the story of one who is truly God coming truly to take our place, and, by taking our place, defining our place both in its ultimate authenticity and its penultimate inauthenticity. The eternal Son

---

[15] *CD* IV/1, p. 240.

assumes our humanity in all its limitedness—not merely the authentic limitedness of humanness but the inauthentic limitedness of our humanity in its sinfulness and lostness: 'God made him who had no sin to be sin for us, so that in him we might become the righteousness of God' (2 Corinthians 5.21). And Christ endures this limitedness, both in its authenticity and its inauthenticity. He endures our finiteness and mortality, he endures our vulnerability and temptation, he endures our suffering, death, and judgement. And he does not flinch. He is tempted to transgress these human limitations in proving his divine identity, he is tempted to flinch from this suffering, death, and judgement in our place. But he does not flinch. He is tempted but he does not sin. He endures.

And to be baptised is to affirm this judgement, is to confess this place, which he has taken and from which he has removed us, as rightfully ours rather than rightfully his. To be baptised is to affirm his suffering and death as our suffering and death. As he identified with us sinners in his baptism and death we, in our baptism, are identified with him. His judgement is our judgement, the exposure of our sinfulness and fallenness, the exposure of our inauthentic humanity. To be baptised is to repent and to be set on a journey of repentance, turning from the inauthentic to the authentic; living under a judgement which now can only be penultimate and trusting in a mercy that is both penultimate and ultimate. The season of Lent is a renewed invitation to repentance, to a turning from the inauthentic to the authentic, but it is also a celebration of mercy; it is a time for renewed self-awareness but it is also a season for rejoicing.

The virtue of 'temperance' tends to be defined in terms of moderation, especially in relation to human passions and appetites, and is sometimes confusingly equated with total abstinence (the spirituality of my youth has a lot for which to answer). Aristotle defines a virtue as a mean between excesses and, consequently, temperance can more properly be identified as the mean between indulgence and abstinence.[16] As I have already intimated, there wasn't much scope for excess in the home within which I was raised. This was partly an outcome of the economic restraints of working-class Britain in the 1950s but more particularly an outworking of a quite strict form of Evangelicalism. We were very good at abstinence but, in Aristotle's terms at least, I'm not sure we were very good at temperance. Which leads me to ponder slightly different definitions of temperance, albeit definitions which can similarly be inferred from Thomas Aquinas' treatment of the theme.[17] To live temperately is to live in a manner that is accepting of the proper

---

[16]   Aristotle, *Ethics: The Nicomachean Ethics,* trans. J.A.K. Thomson (Harmondsworth: Penguin, 1955), II 6-9.
[17]   *ST* II-II 141-70.

limitations of humanness, and to live temperately is to live in a manner in which all desires are ordered in relation to a desire for God, all loves are in relation to this love.

To be human is to be limited, is to be finite, is to be a creature. God and God alone is immortal (1 Timothy 1.17 and 6.16); immortality for the creature can only be contingent, a gift of God rather than an inherent essence. In the story of Adam death comes as a sentence in consequence of sin, but Adam's life in the garden was always and only ever could be a gift, a life in dependence rather than an independent life; Adam is not created inherently and independently immortal; Adam's life is a gift; Adam is created as contingently immortal. But this contingent immortality, this life in dependence upon God, is jeopardised by Adam's sin, specifically by his grasping for more. Contrary to a modernistic preoccupation with bare facts and bare events, metaphor and parable are an enrichment of language rather than an impoverishment of language—they enable us to say more rather than less—and this is specifically the case with the 'Paradise' story, it is rich with imagery that cannot (and must not) be reduced. The difficulty with metaphorical language (if it is a difficulty) is that there is always an element of enigma, significance is never exhausted (though surely this is true of all language). One element (and only one element) of this story of Adam's sin is of a reaching out to exceed a given limitation: the serpent tells the woman (who is not named as 'Eve' until the end of the story) that to eat of this tree of the knowledge of good and evil will render them as 'gods' (Genesis 3.1ff.); whereas God had told Adam that if he ate of the tree he would die (Genesis 2.17). The man and the woman, therefore, reach out to be more than they are and, in doing so, they forfeit what they already have; they become ashamed of their nakedness; they are expelled from the garden; they come to experience pain, frustration, and death; they forfeit an intimate communion with God.

So much of human life is an attempt to 'be as gods', an attempt to cheat death, an attempt to dominate rather than to serve, an attempt to experience what it would be better not to experience, an attempt to live independently rather than in dependent trust, an attempt towards Nietzsche's 'superman' (with little regard to the appalling historical consequences of such attempts).[18] By contrast, when Christ comes as the 'eschatological Adam' (1 Corinthians 15.45), he accepts humanity in all its weakness and limitation, he does not seek to exploit his divine identity, he takes the form of a servant, he is obedient to the point of death, even the shameful death of a criminal on a Cross (Philippians 2.5ff.).

---

[18] This theme pervades Nietzsche's thought, but see especially Friedrich Nietzsche, *Thus Spoke Zarathustra*, trans. R.J. Hollingdale (Harmondsworth: Penguin, 1971).

To be baptised is to abandon an inauthentic humanity with all its vain attempts to dominate, to exploit, to transcend; it is to be re-born into this authentic humanity identified in Christ; it is to accept the way of the Cross, the way of service, the way of suffering, the way of dependence, the way of trust. Lent, therefore, is not simply a season of self-denial or of token abstinence; it is a seasonal reiteration of the invitation and promise which is baptism to be authentically human, to live as servants, to live in dependence, to live in trust. In Lent we journey again with Christ from baptism through the wilderness, through temptation, through rejection, through suffering, and even through death, trusting that the way of the Cross is the way to resurrection and authentic eternal life. To live temperately is (at least in part) to live trustfully and acceptingly within the limitations of our humanness, even within the present limitations of fallen humanness, struggling with temptation, continually dependent upon divine mercy and grace.

To celebrate Lent, then, is to embrace this authentic humanity which is identified in Christ; it is to deny an inauthentic self; but it is not simply and solely a matter of denial: to deny the one thing is to affirm the other. To celebrate Lent as merely a matter of denial or abstinence is potentially distorting. Too easily self-denial can slip into a false asceticism that implicitly repudiates the essential goodness of God's creation. Augustine, and much of the Western tradition thereafter, identifies the root of sin as concupiscence, as disordered desire, but not all desire is disordered desire.[19] All that God has created is created as good; all that God has created is to be received with thanksgiving (1 Timothy 4.3ff.). There is nothing inherently wrong or inappropriate in the desire for adequate food, drink, clothing, and shelter, in the desire for human friendship and human intimacy—such desires are God-given, they accord with the manner in which God has created us within the world. Indeed, all such objects of desire are to be received with thanksgiving as issuing from God's love for us, his care for his creation. Milk, wine, oil, honey, grain, an abundance of flocks and cattle, all are tokens within Scripture of God's blessing, of the 'peace' he grants to his people. Certainly the Bible speaks of fasting as a form of prayer, but it speaks more often of feasting, and the fasting God seeks is never an end in itself but such that issues in acts of justice and mercy (Isaiah 58.1ff.).

And what is true of the desire for food and drink is equally the case with the desire for human friendship and intimacy. In the 'Paradise' story God attests that it is not good for Adam to remain alone and, consequently, forms woman from Adam, effectively dividing Adam into

---

[19] Aurelius Augustine, *On Marriage and Concupiscence*, trans. Peter Holmes, Robert Ernest Wallis, revised Benjamin B. Warfield, in *NPNF1*, vol. 5, pp. 263-308; *ST* I-II 77 5; *Institutes* II i 8.

the male and the female (Genesis 2.18ff.). In Ephesians the love between a husband and a wife is acknowledged as a 'mystery' indicative and reflective of Christ's love for the Church (Ephesians 5.25ff.). And the Gospels attest Jesus, though unmarried, as enjoying the human friendship of his disciples, both male and female. The notion of 'original' sin as 'inherited' sin, transmitted from one generation to another through the lust that is always present in the act of sexual intercourse—a notion detailed by Augustine but at least implied by others before him—is a notion that has afflicted the Western Church (and Western society) with countless miseries, neuroses, and confusions. Our identity as sinful may be inherent but there is no biblical necessity to view it as inherited. Sex is given by God as a means of expressing a most profound form of present human intimacy, an intimacy that is faithfully exclusive but that is simultaneously welcoming of the gift of children. Like every gift of God it is vulnerable to abuse, but like every gift of God it is good in essence and to be celebrated with thanksgiving.

But Augustine was not entirely without a point: appropriate desires all too easily and commonly degenerate into inappropriate desires and, maybe because it is the most profound of human desires and expressive of profound present human intimacy, sexual desire seems the most vulnerable to abuse, perversion, and manipulation. The act of sex may not transmit sin but it often expresses sin; it may not communicate corruption in one sense but it too commonly does so in another sense.

I have considered the sexual relationship between a husband and a wife as the most profound *present* human intimacy but even this qualification is inadequate. The most profound human intimacy is an intimacy that transcends sexual distinction, racial distinction, or any other form of present human distinction; it is the intimacy which we are destined to enjoy with one another as an outcome of our intimacy with God, in Christ, and by the Spirit; and it is an intimacy that is anticipated here and now in the celebration of the Eucharist and in the community that is the Church—it is the intimacy between Christ and his Church that is the deepest present 'mystery'. The highest desire for the other, then, is appropriately an outcome of the desire for God. Indeed, all desires are proper inasmuch as they are ordered to this supreme desire in gratitude.

Thomas Aquinas speaks of the virtues as 'strategies' of love,[20] and consequently temperance can be defined as an appropriate ordering of desire in relation to a love for God that is inclusive of a love for the neighbour; desires are appropriate when they are appropriately ordered to this ultimate desire. Disordered desire, desire that is not ordered by a desire for God, readily degenerates into idolatry, becomes an all

---

[20] Paul J. Wadell, *The Primacy of Love: An Introduction to the Ethics of Thomas Aquinas* (New York and Mahwah: Paulist Press, 1992), p. 90.

consuming obsession, displaces God as the goal of human existence. And such disordered love is inevitably destructive both of the self and of others within an immediate community. To be consumed by the desire for another person, for sex, for food, for alcohol, for money, for material possessions, is ultimately (and often penultimately) to forfeit everything that is truly precious. And to be consumed by desire is to be enslaved; libertarianism is bondage rather freedom; enslavery to desire rather than freedom to desire. To live temperately, then, is to resist this destructive degeneration, is to hold all desires in relation to this supreme desire, is to receive every gift as a gift with expressed thanksgiving, is to be truly free. Jesus pronounces as blessed those who hunger and thirst after righteousness (Matthew 5.6) and promises to those who seek God's kingdom first that all else that they truly need will be given to them (Matthew 6.33). In our celebration of Lent we are invited to join Jesus in the wilderness, resisting the temptation to be dominated by bodily appetites, acknowledging that we too do not live by bread alone, single-mindedly pursuing the Father's will even though it may lead to the self-sacrifice of a Cross. And if tokens of self-denial are at all appropriate in our celebration of Lent, they are so precisely as demonstrations of this right ordering of otherwise appropriate desires, of a disciplined discipleship, of an authentic freedom, of a seeking after God before a seeking after anyone or anything else.

> Almighty and everlasting God,
> who in your tender love towards the human race
> sent your Son our Saviour Jesus Christ
> to take upon him our flesh
> and to suffer death upon the cross:
> grant that we may follow the example
> of his patience and humility
> and also be made partakers of his resurrection;
> through Jesus Christ our Lord…
> Amen.[21]

---

[21] *CCP*, p. 152, and *ASB*.

CHAPTER 5

The One Who Lives And Reigns

Lord of all life and power,
who through the mighty resurrection of your Son
overcame the old order of sin and death
to make all things new in him:
grant that we, being dead to sin
and alive to you in Jesus Christ,
may reign with him in glory;
to whom with you and the Holy Spirit,
be praise and honour, glory and might,
now and in all eternity.
Amen.[1]

Christ is risen!
He is risen indeed!
Hallelujah!

We declare that Christ is risen, but we never declare that Lazarus is risen, or that Jairus' daughter is risen, or that the widow of Nain's son is risen—for the simple reason that they are not risen; they may have been raised from the dead but they were to die again; they rose but they are not risen. The significance of the resurrection of Jesus is not merely that he died and rose again (though he did), nor that the tomb was empty (though it was); the significance of the resurrection is that Christ is risen; he overcame death; he did not merely escape the clutches of death only to die again at some future date; he defeated death once and for all; he lives for ever and eternally. We do not have a word for this, or rather we only have this one word 'resurrection' that we use for these two very different events. The story in John's Gospel of the raising of Lazarus makes clear that, though this miracle was certainly an act of compassion by Jesus, it was not an end in itself, it was a 'sign' of something other and greater; it was a 'sign' of the resurrection of Jesus himself. Lazarus would die again—though, as Martha confesses in the story, he would rise again at the resurrection on the last day. But Jesus, in response to this

---

[1] *CCP*, p. 18, and *ASB*.

confession of faith, declares himself to be this resurrection and raises Lazarus as an illustration and demonstration of this claim. Jesus himself is 'the resurrection and the life' (John 11.25); in him death is finally defeated along with the sin and corruption of which it is an outcome; he is raised to a life that is utterly new.

But this resurrection life of Jesus, though utterly new, is not novel. For all its distinction from this present life, it is also marked by continuity: the risen Jesus is not merely a 'spirit'; he eats and drinks; he has a resurrection 'body'. Contrary to the more crude versions of kenoticism,[2] therefore, Christ is not God–man–God in succession: he is simultaneously and continuously truly and fully God and truly and fully human; he is no less truly and fully God in the manger and on the Cross; he is no less truly and fully human in his resurrection, ascension, and reign; he is truly God as truly human and he is truly human as truly God. The one who prays for us continually and eternally remains truly and fully human; he still understands and identifies with our weaknesses and temptations. As the one who is truly and fully human as truly and fully God he remains our mediator, representing humanity before the Father through the Spirit. Every New Testament reference to the glorified Christ is a vision of one like a son of man, indeed, the resurrected and ascended Christ yet bears the bodily marks of his crucifixion. Through the power of his resurrection every sickness will be cured, every wound will be healed, sin will be removed, and death itself will be defeated—yet the risen Jesus continues to bear the scars of his suffering, not as reminders of defeat but as abiding emblems of this so costly victory. The one who eternally reigns with the Father through the Spirit is and always was truly and fully God, but he is also and always will be truly and fully human—and not just any human or humanity in general; he is eternally this particular man who lived among us and suffered and died and overcame for our sake.

This particularity and continuity of the Son's humanity, though at the heart of Christian confession, is immensely problematic: if he continues in this human particularity, albeit a resurrected and ascended particularity, where is he? Bodily particularity, even resurrected bodily particularity, implies spatial and temporal locatedness. The Bible speaks of the risen Son at the Father's right hand,[3] but where is the Father's right hand? God is spirit, beyond physical, spatial, and temporal locatedness, present in all space and time yet utterly beyond all space and time: but can the Son's true and particular humanity participate in this divine ubiquity without

---

[2] Though there are earlier references, notable in the writings of Count von Zinzendorf, 'kenoticism' is a name given specifically to notions of Christ's 'self-emptying' formulated by Lutheran theologians in the nineteenth century and thereafter adopted (and significantly adapted) by British theologians such as H.R. Mackintosh and P.T. Forsyth.

[3] Luke 22.69; Acts 2.33; 5.31; 7.55-56; Romans 8.34; Ephesians 1.20; Colossians 3.1; Hebrews 1.3; 8.1; 10.12; 12.2; 1 Peter 3.22.

ceasing to be truly and particularly human in any meaningful sense? To be both divine and human is a mystery but to be both ubiquitous and particularly located sounds more like a contradiction. As Paul's discussion in 1 Corinthians 15 demonstrates, the affirmation of Christ's bodily resurrection was immensely problematic in a Hellenistic context with its assumption of a radical and dualistic distinction between spirit and matter: both then and since Platonic and Neo-Platonic notions of the immortality of the soul, notions of a release of the soul from imprisonment within the body rather than the resurrection of the body, have proved both enduring and attractive. But Paul in this chapter concedes no ground to this Hellenistic belittling of the body and materiality: the resurrection body may be other than this present body, it may be a spiritual body (σῶμα πνευματικόν) rather than merely a 'natural' body (σῶμα ψυχικόν), immortal rather than mortal, incorruptible rather than corruptible, but it is still truly a body, albeit a heavenly body (σώματα ἐπουράνια) rather than an earthly body (σώματα ἐπίγεια), continuous and not just discontinuous.

This question of the particular locatedness of Christ's resurrected and ascended body came into sharp focus at the time of the Reformation with Luther's defence of Christ's real presence at the Eucharist through an idiosyncratic interpretation of the doctrine of the *communicatio idiomatum* (the communication of distinctive characteristics). Since the Council of Chalcedon (451) the Church, both in the East and the West (for the overwhelming part), confessed that the single person (ὑπόστασις) of Christ participates fully in the distinctive properties of both the divine and the human natures (φύσεις). Occasionally in the West a more radical interpretation of this doctrine seems to have been adopted—that the divine nature of Christ participates fully in the distinctive properties of the human nature and that the human nature of Christ participates fully in the distinctive properties of the divine nature—and it is this more radical interpretation of the doctrine that Luther employs in his response to Zwingli concerning the real presence of Christ at the Eucharist: since the human nature of Christ participates in the ubiquity of the divine nature Christ can be truly and fully present both at the Father's right hand and at any number of earthly eucharistic celebrations.

While Luther's proposal may appear attractive at first glance as a means of affirming the real presence of Christ at the Eucharist it is, nonetheless, both novel and problematic. It is novel inasmuch as Thomas Aquinas, like Ulrich Zwingli and John Calvin after him, never denied that the risen Christ is spatially located at the Father's right hand: the reality of Christ's presence in and through the Eucharist for Thomas and the catholic tradition is not the consequence of a general ubiquity but rather is unique and sacramental,[4] a specific and mediated presence rather than a general and ubiquitous presence—or, as Calvin would attest, a presence mediated by the Spirit rather than an unmediated and immediate ubiquity.[5] And Luther's proposal is problematic inasmuch as a divine nature capable of all the distinctive properties of human nature no longer could be considered to be truly and simply the divine nature, and a human nature capable of all the distinctive properties of the divine nature no longer could be considered to be truly and really a human nature. Here, surely, we have precisely that 'confusion' of natures and 'change' of natures which the Council of Chalcedon determined to deny; the single and undivided person of Christ is postulated, not as truly and fully divine and truly and fully human without confusion and without change, but as a hybrid, a mingling of two natures; Christ here is postulated, not just as one undivided person, but effectively as one undivided nature.

Calvin and his theological successors were particularly troubled by the implication of Luther's proposal for an understanding of Christ's true and real humanity: humanity participating in all the distinctive properties of divine nature is no longer our humanity; such a Christ no longer comes to stand in our place; such a Christ no longer can be affirmed as being tempted in every way as we are tempted; such a Christ can no longer be an effective mediator and priestly intercessor; such a Christ has no need of the indwelling and empowering of the Spirit since his discrete human nature, participating fully in all the properties of the divine nature, is discretely potent without the need for any presence or power mediated by the third person of the Trinity.

But Luther's proposal is also problematic in its implications for an understanding of Christ's divine nature assuming, as it does, that ubiquity is a necessary and essential property of that divine nature. In the first place, and without prejudice to the gospel story, ubiquity implies spatiality and temporality and therefore, unless we are to assert the necessity and eternity of time and space, we should identify ubiquity as an economic rather than immanent perfection of divine nature. But, more particularly, the incarnate second person of the Trinity is not ubiquitous, he is spatially and temporally located, and—as was noted earlier in this sketch of dogmatics—Christian theology ought to root its understanding of divine nature radically in the gospel story: God eternally is as he has defined himself in this narrative; the incarnate Son is truly and fully divine without being ubiquitous and, since it is this truly and fully incarnate Son who is now risen, there is no reason whatsoever to suppose that this risen and ascended incarnate Son has become ubiquitous.[6]

---

[4] *ST* III 75 1; cf. 76 3-6.

[5] *Institutes* IV xvii 18.

[6] It should be noted, of course, that Calvin's alternative to Luther's proposal, the so-called *extra Calvinisticum*, is no less problematic. In the first place it can be taken in

Corresponding to this denial of incarnate ubiquity, even for the risen and ascended Christ, John Owen, on the basis of a reading of the opening verses of the Book of Revelation, notes that even in ascended glory the incarnate Son similarly is not omniscient; new information is imparted to him from the Father: this is '[t]he revelation of Jesus Christ, *which God gave him...*' (Revelation 1.1: emphasis added).[7]

Nonetheless, though it would seem that (contrary to Luther) we must affirm the particularity of the risen Christ if we are to confess his continuing true and real humanity, this affirmation itself is problematic. It is problematic firstly and most obviously with respect to the difficulty of locating this particular spatial and temporal locatedness. Where is Jesus? Where is the Father's 'right hand'? Writing from within a Lutheran tradition (and perhaps indicating its logical trajectory) Robert Jenson attests Christ as having risen into the Church; the Church is truly the 'body' of the risen Christ and he has need of no other—the glaring difficulties of this affirmation for the maintaining of any distinction between the Church and Christ together with the implicit forfeiture of Christ's authentic particularity I have discussed more fully elsewhere.[8] But in earlier works Professor Jenson proposed a rather different possibility with respect to the risen Christ's spatial and temporal locatedness (a possibility far more compelling, to this reader at least), namely that Christ rose and ascended into the eschatological future.[9] Following Einstein, but also (and more significantly) following Augustine, we should acknowledge time as a further dimension of spatial locatedness: my location as I am writing these words is (very approximately) 51.22.30 degrees North, 0.02.50 degrees West, 90 metres above sea level, and 10.36 a.m. on 27 December 2005—a change of time is as much a change of spatial location as is a change in latitude, longitude, or height. For the risen Christ, then, to be spatially located in the eschatological future is entirely coherent, maintains the integrity of the particularity of his human nature, and perhaps is suggestive of a resolution to the tension between the hope of a conscious being with Christ at death and the hope of a final resurrection—to die in Christ is to participate in his resurrection into this eschatological future. Moreover, for the Spirit to mediate Christ's presence to us from this eschatological

---

contradistinction to Luther as implying a dividing of the single person of Christ, as implicitly Nestorian rather than implicitly Eutychian. But also, in parallel with Luther, it can be taken as similarly implying a divine nature defined behind and beyond the gospel story: it is an essentially ubiquitous divine Son who cannot be confined or defined in human nature.

[7] John Owen, *A Discourse concerning the Holy Spirit*, p. 161.

[8] Colwell, *Promise and Presence*, pp. 80-87.

[9] Robert W. Jenson, *God after God: The God of the Past and the Future as seen in the Work of Karl Barth* (Indianapolis and New York: Bobbs-Merrill, 1969), pp. 157-79.

future is no more problematic, but surely rather less problematic, than for the Spirit to mediate Christ's presence to us from some temporally concurrent location 'above the bright blue sky'. And, similarly, for the Spirit to mediate the unity of the Church, both on earth and in heaven, as a living communion, is no more problematic, but perhaps rather less problematic, if the space between us is temporal rather than spatial (or, rather, temporally spatial). From the end of our history Christ reigns at the Father's right hand and continually intercedes for us. The Spirit mediates his presence to us through the communion of the Church and the Spirit mediates our presence to him, joining our prayers with his praying, enabling us even now to participate in this ultimate communion in him and with one another. And, since Christ thus spatially and temporally located remains authentically particular and thereby authentically human, he represents us as one who still identifies with us utterly, knowing our frailty, sharing our humanity in its created contingency, its limitedness, its dependency. All this, of course, is but speculation—I am writing of that about which I know nothing whatsoever, which is no more and no less than is known by anyone else who writes on these themes—but I write in this manner with the sole aim of maintaining the problematic but essential particularity of the risen Christ, the meaningfulness of the confession of his continuing humanity and priesthood.

It would, of course, be entirely valid to treat the ascension of Christ as a distinct 'season' of the Christian story and within a separate chapter—there would be much to commend this strategy except that I have already committed myself to seven chapters in response to the seven seasons of the Christian Year identified within *Celebrating Common Prayer*, and that Christ's resurrection and ascension (as also his Cross) are brought to a single theological focus in John's Gospel gives warrant for doing similarly here (though the significance of the reign of Christ will be explored in chapter 7 of this book). The risen and ascended Jesus, who remains both truly God and truly human, continually prays for us. Writing as one who has always found prayer hard (and has sometimes found prayer quite impossible) this is perhaps the most comforting assurance of the gospel story: one who remains fully human, who fully understands me, who has been tempted as I have been tempted, who is able to sympathise with my weakness, this one continually lives to pray for me. Moreover, my feeble prayers, for all their misapprehensions and inadequacies, are taken up by the Spirit and incorporated into this eternal and perfect praying of the risen and ascended Jesus who is both truly human and truly God. Prayer, then, is not something that we do to God; prayer is rather that which happens within the life of the eternal Trinity into which, through the Spirit, we are included. No account of human prayer that does not begin and end with the praying of Christ could be considered authentically Christian. The risen Christ does not ascend into the ether of an indeterminate eternity; he ascends to particular spatial and temporal location to continually perform this particular gracious function as our thoroughly human priest and mediator with the Father. The discussion of the risen Christ's continuing particularity is no merely theoretical theological obscurantism, it is pregnant with this intensely personal and practical significance: there is a human ear and a human voice ever present in God.

Questions concerning the particularity of Christ's spatial and temporal locatedness, therefore, are both philosophically intriguing and theologically significant—both the meaningfulness of Christ's risen humanity and the significance of our resurrection hope are at stake here—yet the affirmation of Christ's particularity is problematic for more immediate and foundational reasons. Whatever may be said concerning the continuing particularity of the risen and ascended Christ, the particularity of the incarnate Christ of the gospel story is beyond negotiation in Christian confession. Yet it is this historical particularity— the particularity of Christ as a first-century Palestinian Jewish carpenter and itinerant rabbi, and especially the particularity of Christ as male—that presents an insurmountable personal, moral, and philosophical obstacle to some contemporary theological thinkers. '[I]f the male is God then God is male' concludes Mary Daly as the starting-point for her post-Christian protest,[10] from which objection, with Daphne Hampson and others, issues a rejection of the very possibility of such particularity.[11] What is being denied here is not just the particularity of the Incarnation at the heart of the Christian story but the very possibility of any revelation and defining of God in terms of any particular of creation. God simply, it is here assumed, cannot be such as could be revealed and defined through any created particular. To which the obvious retort is 'who says so?'; from what possible source might one derive this knowledge of what is and what is not possible for God? Or, to repeat again Karl Barth's general retort to all such theistic assumptions:

> Who God is and what it is to be divine is something we have to learn where God has revealed Himself and His nature, the essence of the divine. And if He has revealed

---

[10] Mary Daly, *Beyond God the Father: Towards a Philosophy of Women's Liberation* (London: Women's Press, 1986), p. 19.

[11] '...I deny that there could be a particular revelation of God in any one age, which thenceforth becomes normative for all others... I am simply denying that God (whatever we may mean by God) could be of such a kind that God could intervene in human history, or through a particular person, in a way in which God is not potentially present to us in and through all acts and persons.' Daphne Hampson, *Theology and Feminism* (Oxford: Blackwell, 1990), p. 41.

Himself in Jesus Christ as the God who does this, it is not for us to be wiser than He and to say that it is in contradiction with the divine essence.[12]

Christian faith does not admit the delusory freedom of speculating concerning what might or might not be possible for God. Christian faith confesses its starting-point with this gospel story and strains to grasp its consequences; it infers from this particular occurrence rather than deduces from a delusory general assumption. And, other than in its most trite and puerile guise, Christian faith has never inferred from the particularity of the gospel story that God is male. For God to reveal himself in and through this particular is not for God to confine himself in this particular—the gospel story witnesses not just to the incarnate Son, but also to the Father and to the Spirit. And this language of 'Father' and 'Son', in the context of this narration, is not directly and simply analogous; less still is it simply and generally metaphorical: the terms 'Father' and 'Son' are more appropriately recognized as personal names used between the one who is here incarnate and the one who sent him.[13] And masculine personal pronouns are employed, despite their admitted unhelpfulness, since to employ the noun 'God' as if it were a pronoun is a grammatically awkward affectation (that is hard to sustain), and since to substitute female personal pronouns would be to draw attention to precisely that which is being denied. God, whose image is reflected in male and female is both male and female, and neither male nor female, and beyond all maleness and femaleness.[14]

But the particularity of the gospel story is problematic, not just with respect to fatuous inferences concerning the maleness of God, but for far more common inferences from the maleness of Christ's humanity: the claim that the maleness of Christ implies the maleness of the Church's priesthood or leadership remains depressingly familiar. Indeed, the claim that all humanity is authentically defined in this particular humanity appears inherently exclusive: are we to understand authentic humanity as exclusively male, 'free' (as distinct to being bound in slavery), first-century Palestinian Jewish? As Daphne Hampson herself acknowledges towards the beginning of her criticism and rejection of the Christian

---

[12] *CD* IV/1, p. 186.

[13] For a full account of this argument, see Robert Jenson, 'What is the Point of Trinitarian Theology?', in Christoph Schwöbel (ed.) *Trinitarian Theology Today: Essays on Divine Being and Act* (Edinburgh: T & T Clark, 1995), pp. 31-43.

[14] See Sarah Coakley, '"Femininity" and the Holy Spirit', in Monica Furlong (ed.), *Mirror to the Church: Reflections on Sexism* (London: SPCK, 1988), pp. 124-35, p. 132, referring to Rosemary Radford Ruether, 'The Female Nature of God: A Problem in Contemporary Religious Life', in J.B. Metz and E. Schillebeeckx (eds), *'God as Father?': Concilium* 143 (New York and Edinburgh: Seabury Press and T & T Clark, 1981), pp. 61-66.

tradition, the Early Church avoided this problem by inheriting a lively Hellenistic notion of the relationship between universals and particulars. She assumes, however, that since such an understanding is no longer commonplace it can no longer serve as a defence against inappropriate apprehensions of Christ's particularity.[15] But is this not conceptually defeatist? And is it actually the case that contemporary society has no understanding of universals or of representation? Claims that 'we won the Ashes series' would seem to suggest otherwise. The aphorism deriving from Gregory Nazianzus that the unassumed is the unhealed merely reaffirms and applies the common patristic understanding that the eternal Son assumed this particular humanity as a means of representing all humanity and of redefining all humanity through his life, death, and resurrection.[16]

As Hampson and others acknowledge, that this particular male human being should represent all men and women is no more and no less problematic for us than that this particular Jewish human being should represent Jew and Gentile, or that this particular carpenter should represent all who are slaves and all who are free, or that this particular first-century human should represent all men and women in every age, both before him and after him. Maybe we should note how little is made within the gospel story of Jesus' maleness, carpenter-ness, or first-century-ness. Certainly more is made of his Jewishness but this is then addressed specifically in the New Testament's witness to his radical inclusiveness. The claim of the New Testament and of the faith of the Church is that all humanity, without exception or qualification, is represented and defined in this humanity in a manner that does not abolish but which supersedes every human distinction. All humanity, without distinction, is represented and defined in his death. All humanity, without distinction, is represented and defined in his resurrection.

As was detailed in the previous chapter in reflection on the significance of Lent: he comes to our place of temptation, of sin, of poverty, of corruption, and of death and, in coming to this place, he makes it his own and renders it ours no longer. The particular sinful and fallen humanity he assumes is inclusive and representative of all humanity in every form and in every age. He represents and includes all humanity in his life, suffering, and death, and since Christ represents a woman on the Cross surely a woman can represent Christ at the Eucharist?

But this which was affirmed in the previous chapter is only half the tale of this 'glorious exchange' which is the focal point of the gospel story: he was made sin so that 'in him we might become the righteousness of

---

[15] Hampson, *Theology and Feminism*, pp. 53-58.

[16] '...that which He has not assumed He has not healed; but that which is united to His Godhead is also saved.' Gregory Nazianzus, *Epistle to Cledonius the Priest Against Apollinarius* in *NPNF*2, vol. VII, pp. 439-443, p. 440.

God' (2 Corinthians 5.21); he became poor so that we 'through his poverty might become rich' (2 Corinthians 8.9). In assuming our place and making that place his own, displacing us, he does not leave us without place; he rather brings us to that place which is truly his; by rendering our place his place he renders his place our place. In assuming our place Christ has definitively exposed that place as that of sin, corruption, and death. But in taking that place from us Christ has definitively revealed our authentic place to be his authentic place: he has redefined our true place; he has redefined us. And in this positive sense also Christ represents and includes all humanity: all are included and defined in his suffering and death; all too are included and redefined in his resurrection and ascension. In and through Christ a single new humanity is established that is utterly inclusive: in Christ there 'is neither Jew nor Greek, slave nor free, male nor female' (Galatians 3.28).

For the apostle Paul and for his original readers, of course, it was the first of these divisions that was most pressingly problematic. Indeed, a significant proportion of the New Testament addresses this issue either directly or indirectly and we misconstrue the significance of so much that is here if we fail to recognise the gravity of this issue for these first overwhelmingly Jewish Christian writers. As was intimated in chapter 3 of this book, Luther may well have been right to hear the significance of Romans in the manner that he did, as the basis for a rejection of any 'works righteousness', but it is wholly unlikely that either Paul himself or his first readers were focused primarily on this issue. The question for the text of Romans is not so much how we might be 'justified' before God but rather how God might be recognised as righteous and faithful to Israel through that which has occurred in and through Christ. In Christ God has acted faithfully, rightly, justly, to the point that Christ himself is the righteousness of God.[17] This phrase 'righteousness of God' ($\delta\iota\kappa\alpha\iota\sigma\sigma\dot{\nu}\nu\eta$ $\theta\epsilon\sigma\hat{\nu}$), therefore, more readily draws its significance from the covenantal history of Israel than from Roman law courts and pagan notions of penalty and acquittal. Within the Old Testament the terms 'righteousness' (צדק) and 'justice' (משפט) are covenantal dynamics: the God of Israel establishes righteousness and justice by acting in covenantal faithfulness (חסד), by setting things right, and he seeks that same 'righteousness' (צדק), 'justice' (משפט), and 'faithfulness' (חסד) from his covenant people. That which God has now done in and through Christ, therefore, is not some novelty, it is 'new' in the sense that it utterly and radically changes a situation, but it is not 'new' in the sense

---

[17] As in previous writings, I am grateful to my colleague David Southall for drawing my attention the more probable significance of the phrase 'the righteousness of God' in Romans: David Southall, 'The meaning of $\delta\iota\kappa\alpha\iota\sigma\sigma\dot{\nu}\nu\eta$ $\theta\epsilon\sigma\hat{\nu}$ in Paul's Epistle to the Romans' (Spurgeon's College, the University of Wales: unpublished MTh dissertation, 2002).

of being incoherent or inconsistent. In Christ God has acted with absolute faithfulness to his covenant with Israel precisely by abolishing the division between Jew and Gentile, along with every other human division, and by bringing all men and women, together with creation itself, into covenant relationship with him through this incomprehensible mercy effected and revealed in the gospel.

The sinful humanity that God rejects, then, is the humanity assumed by Christ, taken to the Cross, and terminated there. The righteous humanity that God chooses is that humanity defined by and in the resurrection and ascension of Christ, beyond every distinction of sex, economic circumstance, race, or history. The resurrection of Jesus defines humanity: no other theological definition now pertains. In response to the text of 2 Peter 1.4, the expectation that we will come to 'participate in the divine nature',[18] the Eastern Church in particular (though by no means exclusively)[19] developed a doctrine of 'deification', a notion that can easily be misconstrued or misappropriated. As both Robert Jenson and Douglas Farrow indicate, Athanasius' famous dictum that he '...assumed humanity that we might become God',[20] for all its starkness, should be understood thoroughly in its Christological context: we do not become divine by ceasing to be truly human, anymore than he became human by ceasing to be truly divine; what we become by being united with him through the Spirit is authentic humanity, humanity united with God and participating in God without ceasing to be authentically human.[21] The resurrection of Christ proclaims this authentic humanity to be our eschatological future and our spiritually mediated present. For this divinely participating authenticity we were created. For this divinely participating authenticity we were redeemed. This, and nothing less than this, is the significance of the atonement. This, and nothing less than this, is authentic humanity.

The glaring inadequacy of satisfaction and penal models of atonement in particular, as they have been developed in the Western tradition of the Church, is that they say too little; they fall short of this affirmation of authentic humanity defined in Christ's resurrection. In the case of penal substitutionary models, of course, the fault is more radically and theologically flawed. It is ironic that penal notions of the atonement are

---

[18] ἵνα διὰ τούτων γένησθε θείας κοινωνοὶ φύσεως.

[19] The theme apparently occurs, for instance, in the writings of Thomas Aquinas and John Calvin.

[20] αὐτὸς γὰρ ἐνηνθρώπησεν, ἵνα ἡμεῖς θεοποιηθῶμεν.

[21] Athanasius, *On the Incarnation*, 54; cf. Douglas Farrow, *Ascension and Ecclesia: On the Significance of the Doctrine of the Ascension for Ecclesiology and Christian Cosmology* (Edinburgh: T & T Clark, 1999), pp. 61-62; Robert Jenson, *Systematic Theology*, vol. 2, *The Works of God* (Oxford and New York: Oxford University Press, 1999), p. 341.

commonly employed to justify retributive punishment when it is probable that such penal notions of the atonement (and also of penance) themselves developed in the context of Roman and Anglo-Saxon practices of retributive punishment: covenant law gave way to penal codes, penitence came to be expressed through penalty, a purgatory of punishment overshadowed a purgatory of cleansing, and notions of penal substitution displaced notions of glorious exchange.[22] To date these developments in medieval Western Christianity is far from straightforward but by the time of the Reformation the mutation was all but complete.[23] Those today who challenge notions of penal substitution are often accused of cultural conformity and capitulation, yet historically the matter would appear to be precisely the other way around. As I hope is already clear, this issue is not an outcome of the interpretation of a handful of isolated texts—there are passages in Scripture and in the writings of the Early Church that can be read out of context in a penal sense but there is no necessity to read them is this manner—it is more fundamentally an issue of the nature of God and the nature of divine justice.

As has already been noted, the language of 'righteousness' in Romans and elsewhere in the New Testament finds its probable significance, not in the forensic context of a Roman legal system, but in the sacrificial worship of Old Testament Israel. While the text of Leviticus describes the sacrifices of ancient Israel in some detail it makes no attempt to explain these sacrifices. What is presented is simply the mysterious and costly means through which God maintains Israel as his covenant people in the context of their sin and unfaithfulness. The nearest we come to any idea of substitution (or rather sacramental representation) is in the ritual of the scapegoat (Leviticus 16)—but the scapegoat precisely is not a sacrifice, it represents the people's impurity and a sacrificial victim must be pure. At no point in the text is there any suggestion of a sacrificial victim bearing a penalty: a sacrifice is a gift and an enacted prayer; it is not a means of exacting retribution. Through this sacrificial system, then, God maintains his righteousness (צֶדֶק) and his justice (מִשְׁפָּט) with his people in a manner prospective of an ultimate establishment of righteousness and justice. Justice, in this context, is restorative rather than retributive; it is God acting to set things right, and he acts in such a way out of his covenant faithfulness (חֶסֶד) to his people. And according to the Letter to the Hebrews, these Old Testament sacrifices were but shadows pointing forward to the sacrifice of Christ, the (similarly unexplained) means

---

[22] For this argument in greater detail see chapter 8 of my *Promise and Presence*.

[23] While the detailed argument both of Gustav Aulén in *Christus Victor* and of Timothy Gorringe in *God's Just Vengeance: Crime, Violence and the Rhetoric of Salvation* (Cambridge: Cambridge University Press, 1996) has been challenged, the underlying thesis of these works remains compelling.

through which God now establishes and maintains his righteousness in covenant, not just with Israel, but with all men and women in Christ. His humanity represents all humanity. His death includes and overcomes all death. His resurrection constitutes a new, righteous humanity that is inclusive of all.

A further disturbing failing of penal substitution as an interpretation of the atonement—beyond its implicit division between the Father and the Son, its opposing of divine perfections as if God himself were divided, and its thoroughly non-biblical notions of penalty and justice—is that it inevitably is resolved in a manner that denies this comprehensiveness. The relentless mathematical logic of John Owen's defence of limited atonement is unanswerable: Christ bears the punishment 'either for all the sins of all men', in which case all must be saved since God could not justly exact punishment twice for the same faults; 'or all the sins of some men', in which case only some may be saved and Christ's death pertains only for this limited set of humanity; 'or some sins of all men', in which case all have some sins for which to answer and thereby none may be saved.[24] The common semi-Pelagian alternative to this logical impasse is to deny the completeness of the atonement by positing our human response of faith, rather than the mercy of God in Christ, as the efficient means of salvation: Christ's death is theoretically sufficient for all but actually and effectively sufficient for those who believe (being 'justified' by their own faith rather than by the faithfulness of God in Christ). But this 'self-help' alternative, like the notion of limited atonement it rejects, perpetuates a dual definition of humanity: whether by virtue of their faith or by virtue of individual predestination, some men and women are defined by the humanity of Christ and some are not.

Such limiting strategies signally fail to respond adequately to the universalistic witness of the New Testament to the significance of Jesus Christ: '…we are convinced that one died for all, and therefore all died' (2 Corinthians 5.14); '…God has bound everyone over to disobedience so that he may have mercy on them all' (Romans 11.32). Beyond every human distinction not some but all are defined through the death and resurrection of Christ; not some but all are embraced by the mercy of God through the gospel. Christ's death and resurrection are an overcoming of sin, corruption, death, and all that would separate us from God. In Christ a new humanity—which is, in fact, the original and ultimate humanity in the likeness of which Adam (humanity) was created—is established and defined. And through the transforming indwelling of the Spirit we are, even now, being shaped and formed as this new humanity.

---

[24] John Owen, *The Death of Death in the Death of Christ*, in *The Works of John Owen*, vol. 10, ed. W.H. Goold (London: Banner of Truth Trust, 1967), pp. 140-421, p. 173.

This universalistic scope of the gospel—that all men and women are defined and included in Christ—need not, of course, imply universalism (the inevitability that all men and women will ultimately be saved). We cannot save ourselves but we can condemn ourselves:

> This is the verdict: Light has come into the world, but people loved darkness instead of light because their deeds were evil. All those who do evil hate the light, and will not come into the light for fear that their deeds will be exposed. But those who live by the truth come into the light, so that it may be seen plainly that what they have done has been done through God. (John 3.19-21)

All men and women without distinction are defined in Jesus Christ, who is himself the embodiment of the righteousness of God. But we may refuse and reject this gracious definition; we may, as Karl Barth put it, elect for ourselves the impossible possibility of non-election, of a being in sin and rejection.[25] Overwhelmingly the warnings of ultimate condemnation on the lips of Jesus are directed to those identified as his disciples and, unless we render them innocuous through special pleading, chilling passages in the Letter to the Hebrews should caution us against cheap notions of irresistible grace. We can live in ingratitude. We can live gracelessly. We can live in a manner that rejects this all-inclusive grace of God in Christ. And the utterly righteous God will certainly take this rejection of grace with due seriousness. This divine seriousness might, of course, issue in a mercy that overwhelms our persistent rejection—'I will have mercy on whom I will have mercy...' (Romans 9.15). But, as Karl Barth again insists,[26] such universal mercy cannot be counted upon in advance; it is the mercy of God; it is not a human right; it is not a matter for presumption: this divine seriousness might equally issue in a mercy that grants our persistent rejection eternal validity. But in either case such outcome will issue from God's love which is his justice, not its opposite; God is not divided:

> If the fire of His wrath scorches us, it is because it is the fire of His wrathful love and not His wrathful hate.[27]

The resurrection of Jesus Christ from the dead, therefore, is itself the establishment of God's righteousness and justice, a righteousness and justice that will be brought to fruition and fulfilment eschatologically, but a righteousness and justice which, nevertheless, are effected here, within the course of our human history. The manner of justice here established and effected is not the exacting of retribution, nor merely the restoration

---

[25] *CD* II/2, pp. 315-25.
[26] *CD* II/2, pp. 417-19.
[27] *CD* III/2, p. 609.

of some Aristotelian equilibrium; it is rather and precisely God himself setting things right, revealing, fulfilling, and establishing his own righteousness in this humanity and in our human history. Justice, therefore, is an outcome of God's kingly rule and a characteristic of the 'peace' (שלום) which is the harmony of creation with its Creator. Jesus Christ himself is the righteousness and justice of God, and to this justice we are now called.

The following chapter, with its discussion of the coming of the Spirit at Pentecost, will afford opportunity to reflect on this righteousness as that in which we are now constituted as much as that to which we are now called. A further outcome of forensic interpretations of righteousness (δικαιοσύνη) as 'justification' is the effective forfeiture of an active righteousness in favour of a seemingly impotent divine pronouncement; a declaration that we are righteous in Christ that has little or no immediate practical outcome. Through the mediation of the Spirit, the resurrection of Christ constitutes a people made righteous, actively characterised by gospel virtue demonstrated in acts of righteousness and justice. Such justice, informed by the narratives of Israel and of Christ, is covenantal and relational rather than retributive; it is embodied in ecclesial communities that anticipate a resurrected humanity in Christ through their acceptance, inclusiveness, mercy, and grace. Such justice is positive rather than negative, restorative rather than penal, re-creative rather than judgemental.

Conversely, the demand for justice in contemporary British society (and almost certainly beyond), a demand commonly coming to vitriolic expression through the news media, is almost invariably a demand for vengeance and 'just' retribution. 'I've been denied justice', cries the distraught mother as the drunken driver who killed her child evades a custodial sentence. 'Hanging's too good for him', screams the demented mob attacking the home of a paedophile. 'Justice has been done', claims the triumphant lawyer emerging from the High Court where vast financial compensation has just been awarded against a hospital trust following a bungled operation. For Gilbert and Sullivan's Mikado '...to make the punishment fit the crime' is an 'object all sublime'—but here we encounter satire whereby, perhaps, this entire culture of reprisal is mocked. Not uncommonly the Old Testament's prescription of 'eye for eye' is wrenched from its contexts and cited as justification for such retributive demands—yet there is no evidence within the Old Testament for the actual practice of such mutilation, more probably the text should be taken as commending appropriate compensation for loss or injury, and the context of the maxim has more to do with reparation than retribution. More fundamentally, as has already been noted, Old Testament law (תורה) is covenantal rather than penal; its concern is not 'to make the punishment fit the crime' but to constitute and maintain

Israel in covenant relationship with God. Overwhelmingly in this context, punishment is not a matter of appropriate reprisal for wrongdoing but is rather a matter of purification and discipline. Achan and his household are not destroyed because this is the appropriate penalty for this particular crime but because Achan's sin has contaminated all Israel. Israel and then Judah are given over to exile not because this is the appropriate penalty for unfaithfulness—and certainly not because God, thereby, is disowning them as his people—but because, through this displacement, God is cleansing his people, wooing them back to him, and renewing the covenant. Justice here is a matter of cleansing and restoration rather than retribution and, through the Cross of Christ, contamination has been dealt with, cleansing has been accomplished, restoration has been effected, once and for all. And, perhaps in prospect of this once and for all effecting of justice, Jesus displaces the 'eye for eye' principle and invites us to a life-style of non-retaliation (Matthew 5.38ff.).

The history of the Christian Church is littered with attempts to evade the non-violent, non-coercive, non-retaliatory, non-retributive ethos of the 'sermon on the mount'. Certainly the world, and human society within it, is not yet as God would ultimately have it to be: fallen humanity is characterised by violence, exploitation, tyranny, and injustice. Certainly in such a context, if the poor and the vulnerable are to be protected, there is yet place, regrettably, for limited coercive restraint. But to respond to human injustice with the violence of penal retribution is only to echo and to perpetuate that injustice by refusing Christ's invitation to a true justice that is merciful and restorative. Just War theory developed as a means of identifying criteria for appropriate and limited coercive restraint (and constraint) but it is difficult to identify any conflict that has satisfied such criteria and goals of justice are all too easily confused with aims of self-interest.

In this context of human injustice, then, the Christian Church is called and empowered to live as an embodiment and echo of Christ's invitation to divine justice—not to distorted human notions of justice marked by retribution and vengeance, but to that justice which reflects the character of God by seeking to set things right and to establish peace. To live by this invitation is to resist every temptation to retaliation and revenge. To live by this invitation is to live as a peacemaker, working for reconciliation, reformation, cleansing, and healing. To live by this invitation is, with the apostle, to recognise all men and women as defined through the humanity of Christ, through his death and resurrection. To live by this invitation is to witness to the resurrection, to anticipate a future humanity that is God's chosen and authentic humanity. The season of Easter identifies true justice and calls us to such.

Some early depictions of Christ's Cross, far from portraying a Christ whose head is bowed in death, represent a Christ very much alive, with eyes wide open and head erect, with arms stretched out in blessing more than in crucifixion, surrounded not by a grieving mother and grieving disciples but with spring flowers. Such is the Cross from the viewpoint of Easter. The Cross hereby is an emblem of victory, anticipating Easter morning and an eschatological future rather than a suffering past. In celebrating Easter we celebrate a victory, albeit an inestimably costly victory. It is appropriate to decorate our sanctuaries with spring flowers and the tokens of new life. We celebrate a resurrection and we anticipate a final resurrection to come. But we betray the Easter message if our celebrations descend to a romanticised unreality. In rising Christ embodies a new and authentic humanity, he proclaims a coming kingdom, a realm of ultimate justice and peace. To celebrate Easter, therefore, is to echo this proclamation and to participate in this embodiment. It is through acts of penultimate justice and peace, through our repudiation of acts of violence, oppression, and discrimination, that we truly celebrate Christ's resurrection.

> God,
> through the mighty resurrection
>   of your Son, Jesus Christ,
> you have delivered us from the power of darkness
> and brought us into the kingdom of your love:
> grant that, as he was raised from the dead
> so we may walk in newness of life
> and seek those things which are above;
> where with you, Father, and the Holy Spirit,
> he is alive and reigns,
> now and for ever.
> Amen.[28]

---

[28] *CCP*, p. 32.

CHAPTER 6

The One Who Indwells And Transforms

Almighty God,
who sent your Holy Spirit
to be the life and light of your Church:
open our hearts to the riches of your grace,
that we may bring forth the fruit of the Spirit
in love and joy and peace;
through Jesus Christ our Lord
Amen.[1]

Luke begins his second book addressed to Theophilus with reference to the Gospel, his first volume, as an account of 'all that Jesus *began* to do and to teach' [my emphasis][2]—which, perhaps understandably, has led some to speak of the Acts of the Apostles as Luke's account of all the Jesus *continued* to do and to teach. The first key chapter of Eugene Roger's recent work on the Holy Spirit is entitled 'Everything the Spirit can do the Son can do better' which, though 'tongue-in-cheek', is not a wholly unwarranted response to Western accounts of the Spirit's person and work.[3] Following Augustine's description of the Spirit as the love between the Father and the Son, it became commonplace in Western theology for the Spirit to be depersonalised and for the Spirit's work to be subsumed as the dynamic and continuing aspect of the work of the Son: in late medieval Catholic theology the person of the Spirit is effectively displaced by an impersonal yet substantial notion of grace (a grace which, unlike the Spirit, is all too manipulable by human agents);[4] notwithstanding a few spectacular exceptions (John Calvin and early Calvinism, for instance), the incarnate Christ is perceived to do what he does by virtue of his divinity rather than by virtue of the Spirit's indwelling of his humanity; human sanctification is accounted as an outcome of received grace, a grace imparted through faith and through

---

[1] *CCP*, p. 45, and *ASB*.

[2] ὧν ἤρξατο ὁ Ἰησοῦς ποιεῖν τε καὶ διδάσκειν.

[3] Eugene F. Rogers, Jr, *After the Spirit: A Constructive Pneumatology from Resources Outside the Modern West* (London: SCM Press, 2006).

[4] For a discussion of this reduction and effective substitution see my *Promise and Presence*, pp. 8-10.

the sacraments (the latter being subject to the sacerdotal agency of the priest); the universal reign of Christ is mediated on earth through the agency of the Church (a notion of agency and a notion of the reign of Christ that had quite disastrous outcomes in the era commonly called Christendom); and at the beginning of Karl Barth's *Church Dogmatics* the Spirit is reduced to the 'revealedness' of revelation, the dynamic of the continuing immediacy of the Word.[5]

By contrast, the Spirit as depicted by Luke in Acts is thoroughly personal and prominent: he provokes and he prevents; he inspires and he restrains; all that is done here is done at his prompting; all that is accomplished here is effected by him. Indeed, as Douglas Farrow has argued, the Acts of the Apostles, far from being an account of the continuing presence and action of Jesus, is wholly an accounting for the absence of Jesus—he is at the Father's right hand, he is no longer immediately present and acting—all that he does here he does through the personal agency of the Spirit; his continuing presence and action is mediated by the Spirit.[6] The Acts of the Apostles begins with the repetition by Jesus of the promise of a baptism in the Holy Spirit and, from chapter 2 onwards, all that occurs is an outcome of the Spirit's coming and acting.

Yet to re-designate the Acts of the Apostles as the Acts of the Spirit would be similarly mistaken, would be entirely to misapprehend the Spirit's nature and the manner of his presence and acting. In the first place the Spirit, though truly a personal agent (the 'Lord' in his own presence and acting), acts in a mediatorial manner to the end that, though he remains the agent of divine presence and action, that which he effects can simultaneously be acknowledged as the mediated presence and action of the Father and the Son; the Father and the Son are glorified through the mediating presence and action of the Spirit. In this sense the Acts of the Apostles is truly an account of all that Jesus *continued* to do and to teach, albeit in this mediated manner. But in the second place (and justifying the traditional designation of this book), all that the Spirit effects as the mediating agent of the Father and the Son is simultaneously mediated through the instrumentality of the Apostles and the host of other men and women who are caught up in the service of the gospel. The Spirit's work here, therefore, is mediatorial in two complementary senses: he is the mediating agent of the presence and action of the Father and the Son, yet he mediates that mediated presence and action through human (creaturely) instruments.

This analysis of the narrative of Acts, moreover, is confirmed and supported throughout Scripture; consistently in both Testaments the

---

[5] *CD* I/1, pp. 448-89.
[6] Farrow, *Ascension and Ecclesia*, pp. 15-40.

Spirit mediates the presence and action of God but he does so overwhelmingly through creaturely instrumentality. And, as we should expect, nowhere is this clearer than in the Gospel narratives. Just as every claim of the Apostles is a disclaimer—a pointing away from themselves to the Spirit, and through the Spirit, to the Father and the Son—so every claim of the incarnate Christ is similarly a disclaimer, an acknowledging of the Spirit within him as the means of his acting and speaking, as the means of his fulfilling of the Father's will. Jesus is truly God, this is his continuous personal identity as the eternal Son of the eternal Father, but he is simultaneously truly human and, as such, he remains dependent upon the mediating presence of the Spirit in his human nature. In Luke's first volume addressed to Theophilus, Jesus marks the beginning of his public ministry with reference to a passage from Isaiah:

> The Spirit of the Lord is on me,
> because he has anointed me
> to preach good news to the poor.
> He has sent me to proclaim freedom for the prisoners
> and recovery of sight for the blind,
> to release the oppressed,
> to proclaim the year of the Lord's favour. (Luke 4.18-19)

This, then, is the 'manifesto' through which Jesus, according to Luke, understands his mission and ministry and, albeit by different means, the other Gospel writers convey the same dynamic: the presence and action of the Father are mediated through the Spirit in the human life of the incarnate Son. Luther's idiosyncratic interpretation of the *communicatio idiomatum*, identified and criticised in the previous chapter of this book, not only confuses that which Chalcedon refuses to confuse by conceiving Christ's humanity as capable of all the distinctive properties of divinity, it also, by this misconception, renders the Spirit redundant in relation to Christ himself (and thereby, perhaps, represents the extreme conclusion of the Western tendency to displace the Spirit). A so-called 'Spirit Christology', an account of Christ as a human being ultimately and uniquely inspired and indwelt by the Holy Spirit, is no valid Christology at all since it neglects Christ's personal divine identity as the eternal Son of the Father. But a Christology that renders the dynamic of Christ's ministry and mission as an outcome of this continuity of divine identity, without reference to the mediating presence of the Spirit, is similarly no valid Christology at all since it forfeits any meaningful affirmation of Christ's authentic humanity. Christ is who he is, in his true humanity, through the continuity of his personal identity as the eternal Son of the eternal Father. But, having this identity in this humanity, Christ does what he does, says what he says, and even knows what he knows, through the mediating presence of the Spirit.

And since revelation is genuinely revelation, since God is eternally in himself who he is in the gospel story, then not only must there be an eternal openness in God to the possibility of the humanity assumed by the Son (as intimated in chapter two of this book), there must also be an eternal dynamic of mediation in the relatedness of Father, Son, and Spirit—or, rather, the mediated relatedness narrated in the gospel story is the reiteration in our human history of a mediation in the eternal relatedness of the Trinity. Rather than the (inevitably impersonal) love binding Father and Son in eternal unity, the Spirit, as identified in the gospel story, is the personal mediator of that love between the Father and the Son, not only binding Father and Son together with himself in perfect unity but also (as intimated in chapter 2 of this book) maintaining Father and Son together with himself as distinct trinitarian identities (or persons)—since love that is both absolute and unmediated would tend to collapse into the indistinct monadic singularity. And, as the eternal mediator of this divine love between the Father and the Son who, even in eternity, is never other than the one who takes human flesh, the Holy Spirit is himself the possibility of the mediation of this divine love to and in that which is other than God. Who the Holy Spirit is in the gospel story he is in the eternal communion of God's triune life. Who the Holy Spirit is in the eternal life of God is reiterated and enacted in the gospel story. The story of Pentecost, therefore, is a reiteration and an outworking of the Spirit's eternal identity in relation to the Church in its mission to the world.

Since the rise of the Pentecostal Movement at the beginning of the twentieth century, and the subsequent rise of the Charismatic Movement later that century, affecting established Christian denominations, readings of these chapters in Acts (and, indeed, of other passages of the New Testament) have tended to focus on felt experience and ecstatic manifestation. This, of course, is not unwarranted: the coming of the Spirit upon the disciples on the day of Pentecost was marked with a sound like a rushing wind and the appearance of tongues of flame like fire; the disciples began to praise God in strange languages and the crowds gathered in Jerusalem for the feast understood what was being said; many were visibly affected through Peter's preaching, and the subsequent days, months, and years were marked by some extraordinary miraculous events. All this, of course, is entirely coherent with the Spirit's eternal identity: he does what he does through creaturely instrumental means, through the sound of wind and the appearance of fire, through human praise and ecstasy, through human affectedness and response. But all this, exciting and intriguing as it might be, is secondary, the outward manifestation and outworking of the radically new thing the Spirit is bringing to actuality. Tongues and prophecies, healings and miraculous signs, the ecstatic manifestations and felt experiences recorded in Acts and repeated throughout the history of the Church, are both signs and means of the gathering and separation of the Church by the Spirit and, as such, they ought not to be lightly dismissed or belittled, but neither ought they to be sought or misconstrued as ends in themselves: they are signs and means—secondary signs and secondary means—of this gathering by the Spirit.

As on the day of Pentecost, the principle means through which the Church is gathered by the Spirit are Word and sacrament. In response to the bewilderment of the crowd at the ecstasy of the disciples, Peter proclaims Christ—all authentic Christian preaching, beyond moralistic instruction and motivational exhortation, is a proclamation of Christ—and such proclamation occurs under a promise of God and as a means of the Spirit's mediating presence. That which is recorded here by Luke, in human terms, is not especially eloquent or persuasive, but it is an effective means of the Spirit's convincing presence and, for this reason and this reason alone, it is fruitful. True to his eternal identity, the Spirit mediates the reality of the risen Christ through the human words of Peter's preaching. And those who respond to this preaching in repentance are baptised, not merely as an outward sign of their new found faith but, again, under a promise of God that this baptism in water will issue in a baptism in the Spirit; in an indwelling that is transformative; in a rebirth in relationship to the risen Christ and to all who, similarly through baptism, are united to him; in an empowering to live as witnesses and embodiments of the gospel story. And those so gathered through baptism, who continue to be nurtured through the apostles' teaching, continue also to be nurtured through the communion of the breaking of bread and prayer.[7] Through the means of bread and wine, the Holy Spirit communicates the risen Christ to the Church and through this communication mediates to the Church an anticipation of its eschatological participation in God and, thereby, in one another. Jesus does not pray simply that his Church might be one so that the world might believe—he prays that his Church might be one as he is one with the Father and the Father is one with him; he prays that his Church might be one in the Father and in himself. The unity of the Church is not grounded in the social dynamic of merely human interaction; our unity with one another derives from our unity in God, and our unity in God (and thereby our unity with one another) is mediated by the Spirit through holy baptism and holy communion.

---

[7] Note this possibility of interpreting the text of Acts 2.42 in terms of a list of two (or three) characteristics rather than four: ἦσαν δὲ προσκαρτεροῦντες τῇ διδαχῇ τῶν ἀποστόλων καὶ τῇ κοινωνίᾳ, τῇ κλάσει τοῦ ἄρτου καὶ ταῖς προσευχαῖς.

Jesus, of course, does pray that his Church might be one in order that the world might believe that he was sent by the Father—and any continuing disunity in Christ's Church is a scandalous apostasy and denial of the Church's authentic essence—but any attempt to seek that unity in order to be able to share in communion is disingenuous and futile, a radical confusion of means and ends: the specific unity for which Christ prays is not the means to the end of communion; communion rather is the means (the only means) to the end of the specific unity for which Christ prays. It is through the means of communion that the Holy Spirit mediates to us both our unity with the Father and the Son and our derivative unity with one another.

And since Word and sacrament are no mere empty rituals, the gathering of the Church by the Spirit through these means is transformative. Through Word and sacrament the Holy Spirit draws us into the narrative of the gospel story in a manner that confronts us, humbles us, challenges us, assures us, and changes us. Through our participation in these means and through our participation in one another we are shaped and transformed as a people who themselves, singly and together, reflect the grace of God and, through the Spirit's indwelling and mediation, can ourselves be means of that grace to others. Needless to say, this process of transformation (or sanctification) is slow and not without its setbacks: sometimes through moments of personal crisis, but more often by imperceptible steps, we are being changed by the mediated love of God to be mediators of that love. And because this transformation is a continuing process, the Holy Spirit works through other sacramental means to bring it to fruition: through processes of confession and restoration; through healing and renewal; through the example and encouragement of those to whom we are joined in the fellowship of the Church; and through those ministers who themselves have been called and separated to be instrumental means of grace—through all such and more the Spirit mediates transforming grace to those he is gathering from the world, notwithstanding their distinctions and differences.

As the passage from Joel cited in Peter's Pentecost sermon proclaims, this Church, gathered by the Spirit through Word and sacrament, includes old and young, men and women, slave and free. As the story narrated in Acts unfolds those first disciples discover, albeit painfully and reluctantly, that (far more radically) 'all people' includes Gentiles as well as Jews. The Church is inclusive of all because the gospel is inclusive of all. All humanity is defined beyond all distinction in the humanity of Christ—Jew and Greek, slave and free, male and female—there is and there can be no other valid definition of humanity, and it is the task of the Spirit to actualise this humanity by gathering and separating this Church as witness to this gospel and as first-fruits of its effects.

The Christian Church, then, gathered, separated, and indwelt by the Holy Spirit, becomes itself a living narrative of the gospel, a living anticipation of its final eschatological fulfilment. In a community where there is neither Jew nor Greek, slave nor free, male nor female, in a community where every human distinction is superseded, the single true humanity identified and defined in Christ is reflected and anticipated. In a community being shaped by the indwelling Spirit in the virtues of love, faith, and hope, of temperance, justice, prudence, and fortitude, the character of Christ is reflected and anticipated. In a community empowered by the indwelling Spirit as witness to the gospel story, through its proclamation of that story, through its sacramental indwelling and rendering of that story, through acts of healing, forgiveness, and reconciliation, the kingly reign of Christ is reflected and anticipated. All this, of course, is in process: this is not empty idealism (there never was and there never will be an ideal Church in which all this is perfectly fulfilled) and it is not in the least gainsaid by the faltering and failing reality of the Church in its disunity, sin, and incompleteness—indeed, the disunity, sin, and incompleteness of the Church, for all their tragedy, themselves bear witness to the grace and mercy at the heart of the Christian story. Besides which, the Christian Church is indwelt and being shaped by the Spirit in a yet hostile context in which its defining story is not yet heard and believed but is resisted and rejected. The Church is called to faithfulness in this context but it is in this context that it is called to faithfulness—it does not have the authority or power to change its context, to assume the kingdoms of this world as the kingdom of God. The Church's anticipation of this eschatological future, therefore, cannot be other than bounded and provisional, its very best can only be its very best in this less than best context. As with the sanctification of the individual Christian, the sanctification of the Christian community proceeds by imperceptible steps and is not without significant setbacks. But, through all its imperfections and the limitations of its context, the Christian community is orientated to this goal through the indwelling Spirit and, through this persistent orientation, the Christian Church reflects and anticipates its future—which is also its past—in the resurrection life of Christ.

And the Christian Church reflects and anticipates this eschatological future, not as an end in itself or merely for itself, nor merely as a witness of this eschatological future to creation, but rather as the first-fruits of creation and on behalf of creation. The distinction between the Church and the world, between belief and unbelief, between apparent present response and apparent present rejection and resistance, should never be misconstrued as identical to the distinction between the elect and the reprobate, the ultimately saved and the ultimately unsaved. The Holy Spirit indwells the Church, not for the Church's sole benefit nor as an end in itself, but in order that the Church may be a witness and a sign of creation's own future and calling. All humanity is identified and defined in the single authentic humanity of Christ: there is no other authentic humanity alongside or in contrast to this humanity. God has no other purpose for creation or calling to creation than that which is identified in the gospel story, in the Spirit-mediated communion between the Father and the incarnate Son. It is the Father's purpose that all creation, without ceasing to be creation, without ceasing to be other than God, participates in communion with God in the Son and through the mediating indwelling of the Spirit. God has but one goal for creation—that it should be brought to perfect unity in Christ in relation to him—and it is the rôle of the Spirit to orientate creation to this single goal. Therefore, in orientating the Church to this goal, the Spirit establishes a continuing sign and witness within human history to this single goal of creation.

That which the Holy Spirit does at Pentecost in establishing a community as witness to the resurrection and ascension of Christ is radically new but it is not novel. As Irenaeus recognises, the Son and the Spirit, Word and wisdom, are the agents of God both in creation and redemption;[8] there is no division or deviation here, God's goal for creation revealed in the gospel story is God's sole goal for creation from the very beginning. In one significant sense the Holy Spirit comes at Pentecost, in one significant sense he 'is not' before Jesus is glorified,[9] but in another (and perhaps primary) sense the Spirit eternally is and comes at the beginning of creation. His hovering presence brings shape and order to created matter (Genesis 1.2); he strives with humankind from the beginning (Genesis 6.3); it is his breath that gives life to all that is living (Psalm 104.29). And this ordering of creation by the Spirit from the very beginning is never an end in itself; the goal of creation is never other than that goal identified in the story of redemption; or, in Karl Barth's terms, a doctrine of providence is always secondary to a doctrine of election.[10] Unity in Christ in relation to the Father is always the single goal of creation, in the context of human sin and creation's fallenness this goal is accomplished in the form of redemption, but there was never an alternative or more foundational goal. The Holy Spirit's hovering, striving, and breathing through all creation is always with this single aim of bringing creation into unity in the Son before the Father, and he comes to indwell the Church, gathering it and separating it, as a witness and sign of this single goal.

And, in this providential ordering of creation to its single goal, the Spirit remains true to his eternal identity, mediating the presence and

---

[8] Irenaeus, *Against Heresies* in *ANF*, vol. 1, pp. 315-567, IV xx 1.

[9] John 7.39: οὔπω γὰρ ἦν πνεῦμα, ὅτι Ἰησοῦς οὐδέπω ἐδοξάσθη.

[10] *CD* II/2, pp. 76-93.

purpose of God through creaturely means. A scientific account of physical causality, for this reason, never need be in conflict with an affirmation of the Spirit's providential presence and ordering. The Holy Spirit is not just another cause, albeit a higher cause, in a chain of physical causality. Divine causality, though analogous to created causality, is entirely other than created causality. Divine causality is the ground and possibility of created causality without prejudice to the distinct integrity of the latter. God creates a universe other than himself, with its own distinct integrity as other than himself, yet continually and wholly dependent upon him for its existence and distinct integrity. The Spirit, consequently, orders creation to its goal through created means without jeopardising the distinct integrity and creaturely causality of those created means. This may be mystery—we can affirm the words without fully comprehending their reference—but this is what we are compelled to affirm if we are to maintain both the absolute dependence and the distinct integrity of creation.

The mediated presence and ordering of the Spirit within creation, therefore, as other than physical causality, is not accessible to scientific observation and analysis. As is always the case, that the universe is created, with all that such implies, is an issue of faith rather than detached observation or scientific demonstration. But can any observation (or scientific demonstration) be truly detached? The predisposition to view the universe as uncreated, as self-existent and self-sustaining, is hardly 'detached' observation and, in many senses, is as much a 'faith' commitment as any form of theism. The predisposition (and it is a predisposition) to view the universe as created is self-consciously a commitment of faith—but such admitted faith need not render the commitment incoherent or without warrant. To view the universe as God's creation, as the arena of his Spirit's mediating presence, has its own inner coherence and external warrant, albeit warrant that cannot be established by scientific investigation. That which is spiritual is spiritually discerned (1 Corinthians 2.10-16). To distinguish the Spirit's presence and ordering from physical causality is crucial both for scientific analysis of physical causality and for any meaningful account of human responsibility, but this is not utterly to deny the possibility of discerning the Spirit, his presence and his ordering. Or, to put the matter another and more immediate way, to understand the science of germination, the water cycle, the orbit and tilt of the earth and the consequent seasons, need not inhibit thankfulness. One of the canticles often read or sung during the season of Pentecost is Psalm 103: there may be valid scientific ways of accounting for the provision for human necessities and desires, but as soon as we have named such as 'provision' we have implied a statement of faith; to understand scientific processes of healing and nourishment need not (and should not) limit or prohibit praise to this one who forgives, heals, redeems, crowns with love and compassion, satisfies, and renews. There is no Hebrew word in the Old Testament which bears the significance of 'nature' or 'natural': it is God who cares for the land and waters it; it is God who blesses its crops; it is God who crowns the year with bounty; it is God who covers the meadows with flocks and the valleys with corn (Psalm 65.9-13). Too readily we dismiss such sentiments as primitive and naïve—ancient they may be but primitive and naïve they are not. They are statements of faith and expressions of thanksgiving and, as such, they are not one wit inhibited by scientific accounts of the universe. The Holy Spirit's ordering, sustaining, and providing, is mediated through creaturely means. Such creaturely means can be observed and investigated without prejudice to their identity as 'means', without reference to the divine agent mediating his ordering, sustaining, and providing through those means, yet such observation and investigation need not be a denial of this divine mediating agent or of the identity of creaturely phenomena as means.

And through this mediated sustaining and providing the Holy Spirit is ordering the universe to its end, to its unity in Christ, to its relatedness to God. The universe, thus apprehended, is purposeful, not purposeless; it is ordered to an end. Without this affirmation of the universe as created, of course, it is meaningless to speak of the universe as purposeful; all is meaningless; all is vanity. The gospel story, then, not only affirms the universe as created and purposeful, it identifies the agency of this creation and ordering together with the identity of this purpose and goal. As such, a knowledge of the universe as created, and of the nature and identity of its goal, is an issue of revelation, an issue of faith—it could not be the conclusion of supposedly detached observation. But this is not to deny any intimation of this purposefulness, of the identity of the universe as created, before or alongside a knowledge of the gospel story—indeed, the gospel story itself makes frequent appeal to such intimation:

> ... he has not left himself without testimony: He has shown kindness by giving you rain from heaven and crops in their seasons; he provides you with plenty of food and fills your hearts with joy. (Acts 14.17)

The common mistake at this point (the mistake of so much Thomism of the nineteenth and early twentieth centuries but of which Thomas Aquinas himself appears innocent) is to presume such intimations to be 'natural', to be accessible to independent detached reason, to be 'proofs' in an Enlightenment sense of the word. In the first place, there is much that would militate against such a 'natural' and reasoned conclusion: the universe has not yet been brought to its goal and there is yet much that seemingly contradicts such a goal or orderliness; there is pointless pain and suffering; there are signs of regression and decadence; there is the common experience of frustration and futility; there is much that suggests imminent environmental disaster rather than fulfilment. In the second place, human reason does not derive from detached neutrality; we bring our own presuppositions to our investigation and reflection; even if the purposefulness of the universe were to be accessible to independent rational investigation (which it isn't) we are well capable of distorting such perception and misinterpreting these intimations. And in the third place, and chiefly, these intimations are 'intimations': the Holy Spirit is a personal agent and he never can be reduced to an object at our disposal, subject to our manipulative investigation; he actively intimates this goal, it is not simply given to our objective access. What is in view, therefore, is a 'general revelation' rather than a so-called 'natural theology' (which, as 'natural' could be no valid 'theology' at all), though even the phrase 'general revelation' is seriously misleading since revelation, as the active self-disclosure of God, could never be general or non-specific but is always particular and specific. That which the Holy Spirit intimates through creaturely means is the purposefulness and goal of the universe which alone and always is Christ himself as the union of the true God and the true creature, and he intimates such personally, to particular men and women in their humble and sincere inquiry or, often, in their arrogant and careless indifference. The Christ rendered in the gospel story as the unity and goal of the universe is whispered by the Spirit through creaturely means to those whose ears he has opened to hear and whose eyes he has opened to see.

While, as noted previously, these intimations of the createdness and purposefulness of the universe are assumed within the New Testament by the apostles in their commendation of the gospel story, these intimations are similarly assumed in the so-called wisdom tradition of the Old Testament, in many Psalms, in Job, in Proverbs, in Ecclesiastes, and in specific passages of the Prophets (including Joshua, Judges, Samuel, and Kings). In Proverbs particularly, wisdom is personified (metaphorically at least) as the mediating agent through whom God creates:

> The LORD brought me forth as the first of his works,
>   before his deeds of old;
> I was appointed from eternity,
>   from the beginning, before the world began.
> When there were no oceans, I was given birth,
>   when there were no springs abounding with water;
> before the mountains were settled in place,
>   before the hills, I was given birth,
> before he made the earth or its fields
>   or any of the dust of the world.
> I was there when he set the heavens in place,
>   when he marked out the horizon on the face of the deep,

> when he established the clouds above
>> and fixed securely the fountains of the deep,
> when he gave the sea its boundary
>> so the waters would not overstep his command,
> and when he marked out the foundations of the earth.
>> Then I was the master worker at his side.
> I was filled with delight day after day,
>> rejoicing always in his presence,
> rejoicing in his whole world
>> and delighting in the human race. (Proverbs 8.22-31)

This is poetry and its particulars with reference to a New Testament rendering of the Trinity should not be over-pressed. Nonetheless it is interesting to note that, whereas the Alexandrian tradition of the Early Church tended to interpret personified wisdom as the Word, as the pre-incarnate Son, the Antiochene tradition tended rather to associate wisdom with the Spirit and, in consequence of wisdom here being personified as female and the Greek word for 'wisdom' ($\sigma o \phi i \alpha$) being feminine, frequently referred to the Spirit as 'she'.[11] The danger of the Alexandrian tendency, of course, is once again to subsume any agency of the Spirit under the agency of the Son—it is difficult to discern any meaningful place remaining to the Spirit in creation within this schema. Yet the advantage of the Alexandrian tendency is to clarify that which the Antiochene tendency might obscure: that the Spirit is not self-referring but witnesses always to the Son; that the Son rather than the Spirit is the content and object of true wisdom. Correspondingly, the Antiochene tradition courts the danger of positing the Spirit as the object as well as the agential means of wisdom with the consequent danger of separating the Spirit from the Son, the means from the end. Yet the clear advantage of the Antiochene tradition, as illustrated by Irenaeus, is that it has the potential, at least, of issuing in a more rounded, balanced, and thoroughly trinitarian perception. The wisdom tradition of the Old Testament prompts an understanding of the Spirit as the agent of wisdom within creation, as the one who, through creaturely means, witnesses to the goal of creation, witnesses already to the one who will be disclosed in the gospel story. It is the Spirit who, through creaturely means, invites the simple (those who lack understanding) to come to gain prudence and understanding, knowledge and discretion (Proverbs 8.1-21):

---

[11] In response to the witness of Scripture, there is at least as good a reason to refer to the Spirit as 'she' as 'he'. It would be attractive to adopt this rival and increasingly common convention but, in the context of the Western tradition, to do so courts the danger of drawing attention to precisely that which ought to be denied: God, the one who eternally is Father, Son, and Spirit, is not gendered; he is beyond maleness and femaleness.

Now then, my sons, listen to me;
> blessed are those who keep my ways.
Listen to my instruction and be wise;
> do not ignore it.
Blessed are those who listen to me,
> watching daily at my doors,
> waiting at my doorway.
For those who find me find life
> and receive favour from the LORD.
But those who fail to find me harm themselves;
> all who hate me love death. (Proverbs 8.32-36)

Wisdom, thus identified, cannot be found simply by searching, by detached investigation, or by critical analysis of observable phenomena — yet precisely through such observable phenomena, as creaturely means, the Holy Spirit whispers that true wisdom is 'the fear of the LORD' (Job 28.12-28). The intimation is there for those who would hear it, yet it is an intimation and no more.

And this intimation of true wisdom comes to the 'simple', to those who lack understanding, to those who are open to learn. It does not come to the 'foolish'. Within the wisdom tradition of the Old Testament, as within Jesus' parable of the two builders (Matthew 7.24-27), the fool is distinct from the simpleton; the simpleton does not know (or rather, does not yet know); the fool knows but does not act accordingly. Thus, as Thomas Aquinas attests, it is folly that is contrary to wisdom,[12] and this recognition leads immediately in Thomas' thought to a discussion of prudence which, following Augustine, is to be defined practically as the 'knowledge of what to seek and what to avoid';[13] as 'right reason applied to action'.[14] Wisdom, thus conceived, is not speculative, theoretical, or detached, not merely a matter of the intellect, but thoroughly practical and ethical, a virtue of character, a habit of practice, a coherence of behaviour.[15] Consequently, imprudence, thoughtlessness, inconstancy, negligence, craftiness, guile, and fraud are all listed amongst the vices opposed to prudence and, thereby, as contrary to wisdom and aspects of folly.[16] The fool is not the one who is ignorant of God but the one who knows God yet acts as if God were not (Psalm 14, cf. Psalm 53). Folly is incoherent living, an incoherence encouraged by the modernistic habit of living compartmentalised lives, of separating belief from behaviour, theology from ethics, religion from politics. The one who hears these mediated

---

[12] *ST* II-II 46.
[13] *ST* II-II 47 1.
[14] *ST* II-II 47 8.
[15] *ST* II-II 47 2.
[16] *ST* II-II 53-55.

intimations of the Spirit, who recognises the purposefulness of life, yet lives heedlessly, is a fool. Prudence, as a virtue, is a habit: it is acquired; it is learnt; it is honed. It is honed as we heed the whisperings of the Spirit through the created order, seeking to live in harmony with the purposefulness of creation. It is honed as we are shaped by the Spirit through Word and sacrament, through our indwelling of the gospel story, through our participation in the Christian community. Through these creaturely means we are brought to a coherence of living, to prudence, to wisdom.

It may or may not be valid to infer some hierarchical ordering of the gifts of the Spirit listed by Paul in 1 Corinthians 12.7-11: the list that concludes with tongues and interpretation of tongues is headed by 'the message of wisdom'.[17] The coming of the Spirit upon the Church at Pentecost is marked by remarkable signs, ecstatic utterances, spiritual elation, miraculous healings, but perhaps the most eminent and persuasive mark of the Spirit's coming and presence is the coherence of living which is true wisdom. The same Spirit who breathed order, harmony, and beauty to creation breathes order, harmony, and beauty to human lives, and through these orderings he witnesses to the goal of creation and of human life which is Jesus Christ. A life coherently and consistently ordered to this goal is lived in true wisdom.

In some orderings of the Christian Year a distinct season of Trinity follows a brief season of Pentecost. Either way, Whitsun issues in the longest season of the Christian Year, the longer period of 'ordinary' time. 'Ordinary Time', both here and between the end of Epiphany and the beginning of Lent, is commonly celebrated by the weekly rehearsal of the canticles and prayers appropriate to each of the Christian seasons, enabling a weekly recapitulation of the Christian story. And this is entirely appropriate since it is through our indwelling of the story in its progression and continuity that we are shaped and formed in coherence with that story. But it is the Spirit by whom we are shaped through the recounting of the story and, for this reason, it may be appropriate to continue to consider this extended period of 'ordinary time' as the extended period of Pentecost.[18] It is the Spirit who comes at Pentecost who mediates our indwelling of this unfolding story and, thereby, mediates our transformation through that story by shaping us in coherence with the one rendered in that story, the Christ who is the goal of all creation. Love may be the principal virtue, the virtue that necessarily includes and implies all other virtues, but it is similarly the case that whoever is shaped by the Spirit in true wisdom, in coherence

---

[17] λόγος σοφίας.

[18] The Sundays of this period generally are listed according to their number after Pentecost or after Trinity.

with the gospel story, will necessarily be shaped in all the virtues: in hope, in love, in faithfulness, in temperance, in justice, and in fortitude, because truly in wisdom.

> Lord, you have taught us
> that all our doings without love are nothing worth:
> send your Holy Spirit
> and pour into our hearts
> that most excellent gift of love,
> the true bond of peace and of all virtues,
> without which whoever lives
> is counted dead before you.
> Grant this for the sake of your only Son,
> Jesus Christ our Lord.
> Amen.[19]

---

[19] *CCP*, p. 57 and *ASB*.

CHAPTER 7

The One Who Invites Us Into Communion

> Almighty God,
> you have knit together your elect
> into one communion and fellowship
> in the mystical body of your Son Christ our Lord:
> give us grace so to follow your blessèd saints
> in all virtuous and godly living
> that we may come to those inexpressible joys
> which you have prepared for those who truly love you;
> through Jesus Christ our Lord
> Amen.[1]

The celebration of All Saints' Day is rare amongst Baptists, indeed, evangelical Protestants more generally tend to avoid reference to the 'saints' in the catholic sense of the term, employing the word more generally (and often quaintly) with reference to all Christians. Probably the only awareness of the festival popularly amongst Evangelicals is in response to the commercialisation and distortion that is 'Halloween', but an acknowledgement of the Christian festival itself, or indeed of the festivals of any of the 'saints', is rare amongst evangelical Protestants.

At a popular level this neglect is probably rooted simply in reaction to what are perceived (by Evangelicals) to be the excesses of the cult of some saints amongst Roman Catholics—Evangelicals generally are repulsed by morbid relics and instinctively repudiate the notion of praying to anyone other than God. More fundamentally, however, this neglect probably derives from Reformation disputes concerning the doctrine of purgatory, the authority of the Church (to declare someone a 'saint'), the nature of merit, and an expectation for realised practical holiness. As the Reformation proceeded, so a (proper) emphasis on original sin tended to degenerate amongst some Protestants into a thoroughly negative expectation regarding the possibility of spiritual growth or practical holiness. When John Wesley, true to his High Church roots as much as to the influence of Moravian pietism, championed the

---

[1] *CCP*, p. 164, and *The Promise of His Glory* (London: Church House Publishing and Mowbray, 1991).

possibility of a perfecting of love in a Christian disciple, his ideas were dismissed as idiosyncratic and perverse rather than recognised as the catholic orthodoxy which, in fact, they were and are.[2]

It is not, however, that evangelical Protestantism lacks its heroes of faith: from Foxe's *Book of Martyrs*—devoured with almost equal zeal to Scripture in early Protestant England[3]—through to popular accounts of the lives of Martin Luther and John Calvin, of John Wesley and George Whitefield, of William Wilberforce, of J. Hudson Taylor and C.T. Studd, of C.H. Spurgeon, Evangelicalism thrives on popular biography (some of it of a quite uncritical nature). Moreover, the eagerness of some to acquire items used by Wesley, or notes made in Spurgeon's hand, suggests that Evangelicalism has its own distinctive relics, treasured if not venerated. And, whatever may or may not be an expectation for growth in grace, the motivation for this reverential interest is the desire for worthy example. We need our spiritual heroes; we need our spiritual examples; we need those who encourage us in the hope that a consistent discipleship is possible; we need those whose own spiritual consistency is commended to us by the testimony of history. Jesus alone, of course, is the definition of true humanity, but Paul urges the Corinthians to follow his example as he follows the example of Christ.[4] And all but the most bigoted of evangelical Protestants would acknowledge such examples beyond the boundaries of Evangelicalism; would recognise the example of Mother Theresa and Brother Roger alongside the example of Billy Graham and Martin Luther King; would respect the self-sacrifice of Francis Xavier just as they respect the self-sacrifice of William Carey; and would be impressed by the transparency and simplicity of Francis of Assisi or Catherine of Sienna. All but one of those cited is dead (Brother Roger was killed while this book was being written) but all are commended for the consistency of their Christian witness through historical testimony. None would themselves (I suspect) have claimed perfection, and most would have been horrified by the ascription of 'saint' as a title, but all sought humbly to follow the example of Christ and, as such, all validly are examples to us—and the more we know of their lives, of their

---

[2] For an extended discussion of these trends in evangelical Protestantism see my *Living the Christian Story*, especially chapters 3 and 7; for a more specific discussion of Wesley's place in the catholic tradition see Herbert McGonigle's excellent *Sufficient Saving Grace: John Wesley's Evangelical Arminianism* (Carlisle: Paternoster Press, 2001), or my essay 'Offending in Many Things: A Comparison of John Wesley and Thomas Aquinas on the Nature of Sin in the Believer', in Paul Taylor (ed.), *Wesley Papers: Papers presented to The Wesley Fellowship Conference in 2000* (Ilkeston: The Wesley Fellowship, 2002), pp. 3-14.

[3] John Foxe, *The Book of Martyrs* (London: Thomas Kelly, 1811)—a series of editions and revisions were first published in the mid-sixteenth century.

[4] μιμηταί μου γίνεσθε καθὼς κἀγὼ Χριστοῦ (1 Corinthians 11.1).

weaknesses and struggles as much as of their effectiveness and courage, the more poignant and powerful the example.

In the final chapter of the Letter to the Hebrews the writer urges us to 'remember' our 'leaders', those 'who spoke the word of God' to us, to 'consider the outcome of their way of life', and to 'imitate their faith'.[5] The text then speaks of Jesus Christ as the one who is 'the same yesterday and today and for ever'. Overwhelmingly the leadership commended in the New Testament is the leadership of example: through such examples, demonstrated by the outcome of these lives, the living Word of God is 'spoken' again to us and the changeless Jesus is re-presented to us.

Earlier in this Letter the writer lists those who, in the history of Israel, were examples of faith and of faithfulness (Hebrews 11.1-40). We sometimes refer to this chapter as a list of the heroes of faith but 'heroes', neither here nor elsewhere, is the appropriate word: it is not that they were heroic but that they were faithful; certainly they were courageous but primarily they were obedient; maybe 'saints' is a more appropriate word than 'heroes' since, for all their failings (and some were guilty of significant 'failings'), they were wholly separated to God's call on their lives. Holiness, thus understood, is never legalistic; it is primarily a positive virtue rather than primarily a lack of negative vice; it is a commitment of trustful and faithful openness to God rather than a preoccupation with the avoidance of error or of that which might defile. Jesus is never more holy than when he is healing the sick on the Sabbath or enjoying a party with Levi and his disreputable friends.

So when the writer comes, at the beginning of the next chapter, to speak of these 'faithful ones' as a 'great cloud of witnesses' surrounding us,[6] he could simply be emphasising that we have this host of examples to emulate: here were those who, in their own time and according to their own understanding, trusted God and sought to live faithfully and truthfully, often at significant personal cost and with great courage; as such they represent a 'hall of fame', a gallery of examples to emulate; considering their example urges us to similar trustfulness, faithfulness, and courage.

But the author might be intending an additional idea: it is at least possible to interpret the term 'witnesses' here, not as signifying witnesses of faithfulness to God, but as witnesses of our present faithfulness. The picture then becomes one of an arena in which we are running 'the race marked out for us', with this multitude of faithful ones who have run

---

[5] Μνημνεύετε τῶν ἡγουμένων ὑμῶν, οἵτινες ἐλάλησαν ὑμῖν τὸν λόγον τοῦ θεοῦ, ὧν ἀναθεωροῦντες τὴν ἔκβασιν τῆς ἀναστροφῆς μιμεῖσθε τὴν πίστιν (Hebrews 13.7).

[6] Τοιγαροῦν καὶ ἡμεῖς τοσοῦτον ἔχοντες περικείμενον ἡμῖν νέφος μαρτύρων (Hebrews 12.1).

before us, now urging us on.[7] Such a depiction prompts the notion of a continuing conscious presence of those who have gone before: they are observers of us as much as examples to us; in some sense, albeit remotely, they remain involved with us, and may even remain dependent upon us since 'only together with us would they be made perfect'.[8]

A similar possibility is evoked by the imagery of the Book of Revelation in which, at several points, the boundary between the earth and the heavens is rendered blurred: 'the souls of those who had been slain because of the word of God and the testimony they had maintained' cry to the Lord 'how long' in response to the destruction being brought upon the earth (Revelation 6.9-11); the 'prayers of all the saints' rise up with incense before God (Revelation 8.3-5); those redeemed from the earth as its first-fruits join in the praises of heaven with a new song (Revelation 14.1-5). Albeit figuratively, the 'saints' on earth are bound together with the saints in the heavens as one people, a single congregation, a continuous communion. And though all this is admittedly highly figurative, it surely is significant of something, of a division apparent to us that is less apparent to God.

Such prompted speculations raise a parallel question to that addressed in chapter 5 concerning the 'location' of the ascended Christ: if the 'saints' who have died are in conscious communion with God and yet still comprise a single communion with us, where are they? And as in chapter 5, 'above the bright blue sky' will no more satisfy than 'on the planet Zog'. As in the case of the yet truly human Jesus, perhaps the most persuasive response is that the 'saints' have already been raised with Christ into the eschatological future but that, together with him, their presence is mediated to us by the Spirit and we, by the same Spirit, are caught up in communion with them. And just as our prayers are included by the Spirit in the eternal intercession of Christ, so their praying too (if the imagery of Revelation is to be accepted) is joined with our intercession and included in his. There is, then, but one dynamic and mediated communion of saints, anticipated in prayer and in the Eucharist (where we celebrate our corporate inclusion in Christ), and fulfilled in the eschatological future of final resurrection. Prayer and the celebration of the Eucharist mediate to us in the present that ultimate communion with God into which we, together with all men and women, are invited.

The question, I suspect, at least for evangelical Protestants, is that of the degree to which this single mediated communion is a conscious communion: to what degree might it be appropriate for us to be

---

[7] See, for instance, Harold W. Attridge, *A Commentary on the Epistle to the Hebrews* (ed. Helmut Koester; Philadelphia, PA: Fortress Press, 1989), pp. 354-56; David A. deSilva, *Perseverance in Gratitude: A Socio-Rhetorical Commentary on the Epistle "to the Hebrews"* (Grand Rapids, MI: Eerdmans, 2000), pp. 425-430.

[8] ἵνα μὴ χωρὶς ἡμῶν τελειωθῶσιν (Hebrews 11.40).

conscious of the mediated presence of the saints (or of our anticipated presence with them) in our celebration of the Eucharist; to what degree might it be appropriate for us to be conscious of the praying of the saints alongside our praying (or of our praying being alongside their praying) as mediated by the Spirit in the eternal intercession of Christ; to what degree and in what sense might this single communion imply the possibility of communication, of 'prayers' to the saints or of 'visions' of their mediated presence? And, anticipating continuing disagreement here, is such disagreement an issue of truth and error or rather an issue of what may be deemed helpful or unhelpful? One does not have to transgress the boundaries of Puritanism to find intimations of a conscious mediated communion:

> He wants not friends that hath Thy love,
>   And may converse and walk with Thee,
> And with Thy saints here and above,
>   With whom for ever we must be.
>
> In the communion of Thy saints
>   Is wisdom, safety, and delight;
> And when my heart declines and faints,
>   'Tis raisèd by their heat and light.
>
> ...
>
> Before Thy throne we daily meet
>   As joint petitioners to Thee;
> In spirit we each other greet,
>   And shall again each other see.
>
> The heavenly hosts, world without end,
>   Shall be my company above;
> And Thou, my best and surest friend,
>   Who shall divide me from Thy love?[9]

I suspect that, for evangelical Protestants, the more problematic Catholic practice is that of praying *for* the saints, since the practice would seem to imply a doctrine of purgatory, a process of sanctification continuing beyond death. Such a notion of a process of sanctification beyond death is, of course, not without its biblical warrant (1 Corinthians 3.10-15), and I have defended the idea elsewhere as more biblically and

---

[9] Richard Baxter (1615–91), quoted from *The Baptist Hymn Book* (London: Psalms and Hymns Trust, 1962), no. 360.

theologically coherent than some 'popular' notions of eternal judgement.[10] But, more anecdotally, the practice of praying *for* the saints is instinctive and need imply no formal doctrine of future cleansing. Raised in a devout evangelical home, I was taught to pray from infancy, yet the first spontaneous (and unprogrammed) prayer I can recall praying was, at the age of six, on hearing the news of the death of a favourite great-aunt: 'Lord Jesus, please look after her'—which I suppose is the equivalent of '*Pie Jesu, Domine, dona eis sempiternam requiem*'. If the Spirit mediates genuine communion between the saints it is quite unthinkable that either one should be careless of the other.

Only by virtue of such mediated unity, surely, can the Church truly be deemed the Church at all. The Church *is* the communion of the saints, the community of those, then and now, who participate in the Son by the Spirit. Here and now we are invited to participate, through the mediating presence of the Spirit and alongside those who have gone before us, in the triune communion and conversation of heaven. And precisely through our participation in this mediated communion we are being transformed, we are being shaped as 'saints', as those being made holy through their mediated participation in Christ and in one another. Alongside and through its sharing in the Word and the sacraments, the Church itself is an instrumental means of transformation; through our sharing in one another now and across the centuries we share in Christ and are being shaped in his likeness; the communion of the saints is itself the means through which the saints are identified and formed.

As argued previously, the oneness of the Church cannot be reduced to the merely local, nor can it be attained through ecumenical committees or mere confessional agreement: the true oneness of the Church is mediated by the Spirit through baptism, Eucharist, and ministry in a manner that transcends every supposed distinction of race, sex, or class, of temporal or spatial location. True catholicity is spiritually mediated through the Church's sacramental life and consists in its continuity and connectedness across the centuries and universally. Since the Spirit who joins me to Christ joins me simultaneously to all his people, I cannot be joined to Christ without being joined to them. My oneness with Irenaeus, Athanasius, Macrina, Augustine, John of Damascus, Clare of Assisi, Thomas Aquinas, Julian of Norwich, Luther, Calvin, Wesley, Hannah Pearsall Smith,[11] and all the saints of the past—not to mention my father, my grandmother, and all those in my own life-time who have influenced my walk with God—derives from my mediated oneness with Christ and the former demonstrates and signifies the latter. To be careless of this

---

[10] Colwell, *Promise and Presence*, ch. 8.

[11] Hannah Pearsall Smith (1832–1911), with her husband Robert, was inspirational in the founding of the Keswick Movement.

catholic oneness, of this continuity and connectedness through time and space, is to deny the reality of the Church and, thereby, to deny Christ. And, just as our oneness with Christ is established and celebrated through the sacraments and through prayer, so also through the sacraments and prayer our oneness with all the saints is established and celebrated. When we pray, through the mediation of the Spirit, our prayers are incorporated in the praying of Christ and, thereby, are joined with the praying of those who already inhabit his eschatological future, and who urge us on in faithful discipleship. When we celebrate the Eucharist, through the mediation of the Spirit, we participate in Christ and, thereby, anticipate the fulfilment of that communion with him alongside those who have already attained it; by the Spirit they are present to us and we are present to them. Imagination is a much-underrated human faculty, not least within Christian worship, yet imagination of the presence and participation of this glorified company—imagination, that is, of what through the Spirit is the mediated reality—can prove transformative of the experience of prayer and of communion. We are never alone here. We are surrounded by a 'great cloud of witnesses'.

The traditional means of distinguishing between the 'saints' of the present and the 'saints' of the past who have already attained the eschatological future—a tradition I have endeavoured to avoid in this book—is the distinction between the Church militant and the Church triumphant. The distinction, of course, is not wholly inappropriate: the Church in the world exists in a context of active hostility, its task and its struggles continue; whereas the Church glorified has already overcome, its struggles are behind it, it no longer is confronted by hostile opposition (though, if what was said previously concerning the saints' mediated presence with us is valid, even this latter distinction must be qualified: they yet share our struggles; albeit as spectators of that struggle they continue to bear with us in prayer). Moreover, alternative distinctions are significantly defective: to distinguish between the Church on earth and the Church in heaven (a distinction I have employed) encourages notions of a Church 'above the bright blue sky' (though biblically, while 'heaven' can simply signify that which is 'above' us, it can also signify God himself and the location of his perceivable presence); while the Church 'below' and the Church 'above' only renders specific the problem of a mythically tiered universe; and the Church 'active' and the Church 'passive' (or at rest) directly denies the active participation of the glorified saints in the continuing struggles of the 'active' Church.

But the terms 'militant' and 'triumphant' bear connotations that are not just inappropriate, unhelpful, and offensive (especially in our present context), they bear connotations and echoes of a history that is profoundly blasphemous and apostate. Notions of triumph inevitably degenerate into triumphalism; and notions of militancy inherently signify aggression and militarism. And even a cursory knowledge of Church history (or even of the more general history of Western Europe) exposes a Church that too often has been all too triumphalistic and all too militaristic. Militaristic metaphors have vitiated the Church's hymnody and its language of mission and, though rich in some senses, such language remains deeply offensive, problematic, and contradictory: a kingdom of peace, reconciliation, and healing simply cannot be celebrated and commended in such terms. And before someone objects that the New Testament occasionally employs militaristic metaphors they should pause to recognise the ironic nature of such employment: the 'weapons we fight with are not the weapons of the world' (2 Corinthians 10.4); the 'armour of God' consists of 'truth', 'righteousness', the 'gospel of peace', 'faith', and 'prayer' (Ephesians 6.10-18); and, as noted previously, the 'dragon' is overcome 'by the blood of the Lamb and by the word of their testimony' (Revelation 12.11). Time and again the New Testament deconstructs our common and violent notions of struggle and triumph.

The term 'Christendom' is used rather too loosely in some contemporary Christian writing as a self-evident repudiation of the major part of the Church's history with little attempt to delineate what may be appropriate in the signification of the term and what was certainly deeply inappropriate. Consequently I need to clarify that it is not at all my intention to deny or to qualify the Church's confession of the universal Lordship of Christ or the ultimate fulfilment of that Lordship—even though this claim and this expectation may be deemed offensive in the ears of liberal pluralism. Nor is it my intention to repudiate the fruitfulness and effectiveness of the Church in its mission or the hope that such fruitfulness and effectiveness might recur.[12] Nor can I subscribe to the naïve Enlightenment assumption that Christianity is a merely private affair; that belief can be separated from practice; that theology can be separated from ethics; that religion can be separated from politics. If the universal Lordship of Christ, or the effectiveness of the Church in its mission, or the political and ethical essence of Christian commitment are intended by the term 'Christendom', then Christendom is to be unashamedly affirmed rather than shamedly denied. But when the Church, through the effectiveness of its mission and its confession of the universal Lordship of Christ, found itself in a place of secular political influence and succumbed to the temptation to employ coercive and violent means to further its ends (thereby denying and abandoning its authentic ends), then the Church apostatised by denying the nature of the

---

[12] Note Oliver O'Donovan's comment that Christendom was simply the Church being successful in its mission. Oliver O'Donovan, *The Desire of the Nations: Rediscovering the Roots of Political Theology* (Cambridge: Cambridge University Press, 1996), esp. pp. 193-226.

Lordship of its Lord—and this, which is an outcome of Christendom rather than its necessary essence, must be repudiated unequivocally.

The history of Crusade, of Inquisition, of pogrom, of enforced baptism, of violent coercion, of torture, of execution, of every confusion of triumph with triumphalism, of militancy with militarism, is a blasphemous pollution of Christ's body and, therefore, of Christ himself. It simply is not possible to perpetrate such acts of violent coercion in the name of the Christ of the Gospels, in the name of the one who is truly God, in the name of the one who is truly human. While I was writing this chapter a suspected plot to destroy aircraft in mid-flight and, thereby, to destroy not only passengers and crew but also to destroy all in the pathway of crashing aircraft was foiled (apparently) by British Security services. While I was writing this chapter a United Nations' resolution for a ceasefire in Lebanon between the forces of Israel and Hezbollah was finally agreed and implemented. While I was writing this chapter armed conflict continued in Afghanistan and Iraq—conflict which some Muslims portray as a war on Islam, a 'crusade' perpetrated yet again by the imperialistic and 'Christian' West. It hardly needs to be argued, therefore, that in such a tragic context it is prudent to avoid the insensitive language of triumph and militancy. But the issue is more foundational than present political expediency and sensitivity. The issue takes us to the heart of an understanding of the Christ of the Gospels, of the nature of his triumph, of the nature of the true humanity he invites us to share through the Spirit, of the eternal nature of God as identified as Father, Son, and Spirit.

At this point and in this contemporary context an absolute repudiation of violence and coercion becomes immensely attractive but, as I have argued elsewhere, at least theoretically I remain unable to embrace this absolutist stance without qualification (and with qualification it no longer remains absolutist).[13] In the first place, I find myself unable to embrace an absolute repudiation of coercion (and all coercion is violent in a general sense) because, as previously stated, I am compelled to repudiate the common Enlightenment disjunction of belief and practice, theology and ethics, religion and politics. Christianity cannot be a merely private affair, not only because God's invitation in Christ extends to all humanity and the universe itself, but also (and more mundanely) because human life is not neatly compartmentalised, dualistically divided, or discontinuous. We are our beliefs and commitments. Our practices identify our confessions. My confession of the risen Christ is meaningless if it doesn't issue in faithful practices within human relationships. And since this Enlightenment disjunction of belief and practice is entirely delusory, it simply is not possible to legislate for or against certain

---

[13] Colwell, *Living the Christian Story*, ch. 10.

practices without legislating for or against certain beliefs—to do the one is inherently, rather than implicitly, to do the other. To legislate against human sacrifice is inherently to legislate against particular confession. To legislate with regard to the practice of abortion, family life, business practices, or environmental responsibility is inherently to legislate with regard to particular confession. In other words, politics is inevitably and inherently religious and religion is inevitably and inherently political. And since politics, as the attempted (and admittedly provisional) right ordering of society, is appropriate and is inevitably and inherently coercive, legislating both to constrain and to restrain, religion similarly is inevitably and inherently coercive.

But in the second place, and foundationally, the Jesus who calls us not to resist evil (Matthew 5.39) and himself goes submissively to the Cross is the Jesus who made a whip and cleared the Temple court of traders; the Peter who calls us to endure unjust suffering (1 Peter 2.19-25) is the Peter who speaks death to Ananias and Sapphira (Acts 5.1-11). Christ defines the true God and our true humanity to us in a temporal context that is not yet the eschatological fulfilment of all things; a context that remains fallen and sinful; a context that is not yet as God ultimately invites the universe to become by his Spirit. And in such a context for Christ—and therefore for God as well as for us—the absolute best, that which is ultimately desirable, is simply unavailable. Certainly the Church is called to bear prophetic witness to an eschatological future and to anticipate that future in its actions and attitudes as much as its words. But, in a context where that future remains future, there are appropriate and inappropriate ways in which it may be anticipated. Violent crime must be confronted and the criminal should be restrained—but any form of restraint is itself a form of coercion, a form of violence. And societies are as capable of criminality as are individuals, and, consequently, I find it incoherent entirely to exclude the possibility of restraint—even violent restraint—on a societal or international scale. That which renders me a practical rather than a theoretical pacifist is the recognition that notions of justice are inevitably particular and prejudiced, and that even such qualified notions of justice readily (and regularly) become confused with issues of political and economic self-interest. Criteria for defining a 'just war' were formulated as a means of assessing the appropriateness or inappropriateness of violent response—it is difficult to fault or to improve upon these criteria, but it is also difficult (at least for this student of history) to identify a single conflict, especially in recent history, where these criteria have been met and fulfilled.

Yet even when such qualifications have been applied—that confession is coercive because confession is political; that the world is not yet at its eschatological goal and that, therefore, a degree of constraint and restraint remains appropriate—the qualifications are not without qualification: the appropriateness of political legislation is not warrant for tyranny; the appropriateness of necessary restraint is not warrant for unlimited violence; Jesus makes a whip and clears the Temple court but he doesn't drop napalm or send in one of his disciples as a suicide bomber (or whatever the first-century equivalent of such violence may be). He confronts evil but he invites rather than compels response. And, though the cleansing of the Temple is as much a part of the gospel story as the healing of a leper or the feeding of the five thousand, it remains an isolated incident in the story of Jesus, all the more notable for its apparent incongruity. Jesus compels no one to follow him. He rejects the way of violence and self-defence and he calls his disciples to follow after him, to bear the Cross.

All Saints' Day marks the beginning of the 'Kingdom' season of the Christian Year in some orderings of these seasons. Even now the Jesus who has ascended to the Father's right hand reigns throughout the universe and his kingly reign is mediated by the Spirit here and now through the Church. Even now the Kingdom of God is present among us and signs of this Kingdom are discernable to eyes that have been opened by the Spirit. But this Kingdom could not be more different from the kingdom of Caesar and all other earthly rulers: it is not established by violence and coercion but by testimony, by suffering, and by endurance; it is not characterised by imperialism, triumphalism, or conquest, but by submission and by servanthood; its signs are not the emblems of warfare or military might, but lives that are healed, restored, and reordered; the majesty of its King is identified, not through pomp and the trappings of power but through the weakness and disgrace of a Cross. Throughout the Gospels we find Jesus continually challenging popular expectations of Messiah-ship and of God's coming Kingdom, continually deconstructing assumed notions of authority and power. His disciples then and ever since have proved slow to get the point; have persisted in confusing his Kingdom with the kingdoms of this world; have grasped at and exercised hierarchical forms of authority and power; have sought to establish his Kingdom by means that inherently deny it. But that which is authentically his Kingdom reflects and echoes his nature, that nature rendered through the gospel story and supremely in his journey to the Cross. This is who he is then and now because this is who he is eternally. This is truly the nature of God. This is the true humanity he invites us to share.

Certainly amongst those listed in the eleventh chapter of Hebrews are warriors in the common sense of the term, are those who 'conquered kingdoms', became 'powerful in battle', and 'routed foreign armies' (Hebrews 11.33-34), but they are commended for their faithfulness rather than for their military prowess, and their names are set alongside those who 'were tortured and refused to be released', who endured 'jeers and flogging', who were 'chained' and imprisoned, who through all manner of abuse and persecution commended themselves as 'other' in relation to the world (Hebrews 11.35-38). Moreover, the example (and active encouragement) of such is taken up in the following chapter, alongside the example of the endurance of Christ, to urge us, the readers of the text, to 'endure hardship', to make 'every effort to live in peace with everyone', and 'to be holy' (Hebrews 12.7 and 14). Nowhere through this text are we exhorted to emulate aggression, violence, or coercion; that which is exemplary here is the fortitude of endurance rather than the courage of violent confrontation. The saints who lived ahead of us 'triumphed' through their trustful endurance and it is to the militancy of faithful endurance, rather than to any other form of militancy, to which we now are called.

As with any other document of the New Testament (or the Old Testament), we cannot possibly now know with absolute certainty the precise occasion and context in response to which the Letter to the Hebrews was written. Its title, its manner, and its imagery all suggest that it was originally addressed to Jewish Christians, and the particulars of its argument may imply that it was written in response to some such who, growing despondent, weary, or disillusioned in their Christian discipleship, were in danger of re-embracing Judaism and, in particular, the Jewish sacrificial system as a continuing and tangible 'token' of forgiveness (on balance this possibility would seem to necessitate an early date for the Letter).[14] Such an interpretation, while taking full account of the general Old Testament imagery and allusions of the text, accords especial significance to the Letter's extended discussion of the significance and limitations of Old Testament sacrifices and to the warning that 'no sacrifice for sins is left':[15] beyond that which Christ has done once and for all for us there is no sacrifice for sin, indeed the sacrifices commended in the Old Testament were always only foreshadowings of this single sacrifice of Christ. The earliest readers of this Letter, and we with them, are urged not to grow weary or despondent, not to revert to previous allegiances and assurances, not to live distrustfully, unfaithfully, or untruthfully, but to cleave to Christ resolutely, enduring hardship, discouragement, and disgrace. For the writer of this Letter the alternative is truly dreadful: to reject Christ by abandoning trust in him and in that which he has accomplished is to fall liable to unmitigated and unrelenting judgement (Hebrews 10.26-31). No ground is offered here to notions of cheap grace or careless presumption: those who are faithful, those who truly are 'saints', are those who persevere to the end (Hebrews 10.35-39); they may persevere through

---

[14] See, for instance, Barnabas Lindars, *The Theology of the Letter to the Hebrews* (Cambridge: Cambridge University Press, 1991), pp. 4-21; Andrew T. Lincoln, *Hebrews: A Guide* (London: T & T Clark, 2006), pp. 52-68.

[15] οὐκέτι περὶ ἁμαρτιῶν ἀπολείπεται θυσία (Hebrews 10.26).

'preserving grace' but the apparent assumption of this Letter is that such grace is resistible.

The Christian Year, beginning with the season of Advent, begins with hope; with the expectation that the true God who has come will come; with the recognition that we have not yet arrived at our ultimate goal. And, with the season marked at its beginning with All Saints' Day, the Christian Year reaches its conclusion again with this note of 'not yet', with the confession of what is yet provisional and unfulfilled. The glorified saints have gained the eschatological future; they have 'triumphed' through patient and faithful endurance; they have reached the goal. But here and now that goal yet lies ahead of us; patience, faithfulness and endurance remain our present lot and calling. One recurring theme throughout the Letter to the Hebrews is that of pilgrimage: the faithfulness of the people of Israel is tested through their wanderings in the desert (Hebrews 3.7—4.11); those listed as examples of faith were 'aliens and strangers on earth', demonstrating that 'they were longing for a better country—a heavenly one' (Hebrews 11.13-16); and similarly we here 'do not have an enduring city, but…are looking for the city that is to come' (Hebrews 13.14). It is for this reason that we are urged to join Jesus 'outside the camp, bearing the disgrace he bore' (Hebrews 13.13). The invitation to bear Christ's disgrace is hardly an attractive selling-point for the Christian religion, but it is the irreducible requirement of authentic discipleship. Pilgrimage is not tourism (though in our present context we easily mistake it for such): it implies diligence, single-mindedness, patience, faithfulness, and endurance. And, as such, it calls for fortitude which, if it can be distinguished from courage in general, is marked by persistence—courage, though a virtue of character, may be demonstrated by a momentary act of bravery; fortitude, as a virtue of character, signifies a constancy of courage in the face of adversity, it is the persistence of courage, it is endurance.

The Christian life is a pilgrimage, a journey with a goal not yet attained by us though attained by those faithful ones who have preceded us. And, as such a journey, it demands the discipline of patient endurance and the virtue of fortitude. To follow Jesus prayerfully through the canticles, readings, and prayers of the Christian Year clarifies the nature of Christian discipleship as a journey, a journey with a clearly defined goal. Of course, the virtues demanded by this journey, the virtues in which we are formed through the journey itself, are mutually informing and continuous—love is not set over against justice anymore than Christmas can be set over against Easter. But without fortitude, without endurance, without persistence, we shall not arrive at the journey's goal. Those who truly are 'saints' are identified by perseverance.

Grant, Lord,
that we who are baptised into the death
of your Son our Saviour Jesus Christ
may continually put to death our evil desires
and be buried with him;
that through the grave and gate of death
we may pass to our joyful resurrection;
through his merits, who died and was buried
and rose again for us,
your Son Jesus Christ our Lord.
Amen.[16]

---

[16] *CCP*, p. 176, and *ASB*.

Conclusion

Lord, have mercy.
Christ, have mercy.
Lord, have mercy.

This book began with the acknowledgement that it was experimental: though some advantages and disadvantages of considering the themes of theology within the structure of the seasons of the Christian Year could be foreseen the overall effectiveness of the strategy could not be predicted, and the overriding goal of integrating doctrine and ethics, and identifying both as the language and practice of worship, might prove elusive. As was also acknowledged in the Preface of this book, it is for others to comment on the relative success or failure of the experiment and, here more than ever, I need to be attentive to my critics. Nonetheless, having admitted the experimental and provisional nature of the exercise, it seems appropriate that (without pre-empting my critics) I should reflect myself on the outcomes of the experiment.

From a doctrinal perspective, the glaring danger of this approach is that of both omission and repetition: the classic (Reformed) structure of a 'systematics', ordered to the four articles of the creed, has been honed through common employment to the degree that the location of particular themes—of eschatology, of sanctification, of the sacraments, for instance—can be predicted, there is minimal repetition and little likelihood of (or excuse for) omission. By definition, I may be missing the fact that I have missed something but, as far as I am presently aware, this very different approach and structure has enabled some passing engagement with all the major themes of theology—it is the brevity of that engagement that is frustrating and unsatisfactory (a doctrine of Christian ministry, for instance, is identified but never expanded). This, however, is the inevitable outcome of the other sense in which this work is provisional: it was only ever intended as a sketch of dogmatics, an outline of a possible (though remote) future project. Some questions and themes have here been raised in passing that merit a chapter of discussion at least, and to this author (more accustomed to writing more detailed accounts) this is immensely frustrating. As I have admitted before, comprehensiveness is unattainable (far too much has been written for it to be possible to engage with everything) and, in theology, is undesirable: it would be arrogant, foolish, and blasphemous to presume to have said all that could or should be said; incompleteness and admitted inadequacy in theology is a virtue. But where, in this instance, this lack of completeness is most pronounced and least acceptable is in the limited engagement with the tradition that a work of this brevity allows. The work of theology is a conversation, a conversation within the Church catholic that spans the centuries, the contexts, and the sub-traditions arising from (regrettable) denominational distinctiveness. Theology can never validly be a private affair; we are not the first generation to have worshipped, prayed, read Scripture, or sought to follow Christ; we can only validly proceed through a careful, gracious, and sustained listening to one another across the distinctions of time, place, and perception. I can only hope that, even in a work where such explicit conversation is so limited and never sustained, the continuing conversations underlying what is here, nonetheless, are evident.

Given the structure adopted here, the one theme that a casual reading may deem absent is that of the Trinity. In some orderings of the Christian Year, Trinity Sunday marks the beginning of a distinct season which, rather than Pentecost, issues in the longer period of 'Ordinary Time' and, consequently, some would expect me to take this as the occasion to discuss the theme explicitly. The 'omission', of course, is entirely deliberate. Theology in its entirety is the consideration of God and God has made himself known in the gospel story as eternally the Father, the Son, and the Spirit. The doctrine of the Trinity should never be a sub-theme of Christian theology: it is the entirety of Christian theology. This always and only is the one we worship, the one to whom we pray, the one to whose invitation we seek to respond. This brief sketch, for all its provisionality, will have failed utterly if each chapter is not explicitly and wholly a response to the one who is Father, Son, and Holy Spirit.

But this in turn raises the complementary concern of repetition: the structure adopted in this sketch lends itself to the possibility of repetition and, while the whole of Christian theology is properly trinitarian, there are other themes, subordinate themes, that recur in more than one chapter. In so brief a work such repetition may justly be considered a fault, especially in comparison to more traditional orderings of doctrine where such repetition is usually minimal. However (I hope without perversity), I would want to defend this repetition; I do not consider it a fault. Christian theology is not the neat and tidy (inherently modernistic) exercise that some treatments may intimate: since God as Trinity is its sole theme every supposed sub-theme is interrelated and interpenetrating; no single sub-theme can be considered without prejudice to every other sub-theme. Repetition, therefore, I deem to be both necessary and virtuous, an outcome of appropriate integration.

Though I have admitted the artificiality of linking particular virtues with particular seasons of the Christian Year (a strategy motivated entirely by systematic tidiness) the association has, from my standpoint, proved more natural and persuasive than I had hoped. The basic principle, of course, is properly basic: doctrine and ethics are not two themes but a single theme; it is not that Christian confession implies an ethical commitment—Christian confession is an ethical commitment. Moreover, the ethical commitment which is authentic Christian confession is not located in a series of punctiliar responses to a series of discrete dilemmas but in those virtuous habits in which we are being formed by the Spirit through our indwelling of the Christian story, an indwelling mediated through our participation in the sacramental life of the Christian community. Inasmuch as the liturgy of the Christian Year enables a prayerful indwelling of the gospel story, the liturgy itself is a means of ethical transformation, and inasmuch as the liturgy of the Christian Year identifies specific scenes and stages in the gospel story it similarly identifies specific virtues as aspects of the true humanity of Christ in which we are being renewed. I still would not want to claim any intrinsic or necessary relationship between Epiphany and faithfulness or Advent and fortitude, but these associations have been (for me) more evident and more fruitful than I had anticipated. Most importantly, this structuring of doctrine clarifies that Christian commitment is the commitment of discipleship. We are followers after Christ. We are pilgrims. We are on a journey—and this journey is transformative.

The integration of doctrine and ethics, though I am sure it could be improved upon, has been personally instructive and clearer than I had hoped. Where I have found the project most frustrating and inadequate is with respect to the integration of doctrine (and ethics) and worship. Simply to structure an exploration of doctrine and the Christian life according to liturgical seasons itself renders explicit the integration of worship and prayer with doctrine. Yet, beyond this simple structuring and the enclosing of each chapter in prayer, I have found it extraordinarily difficult to sustain as explicit the worshipful and prayerful nature and context of all theology and ethics. I am eager to learn from others how this may be done without descent into artificiality and feigned piety. Theology is the language of worship and worship is the context and manner of true theology. The Christian life is not mere moralism and theology cannot validly be considered in detachment. Yet it is hard to convey this inherent integration, this irreducible character, in a text. Inasmuch as worship and prayer are brought to a text by a reader (or author) rather than inherent in a text maybe my hope is unattainable (though I suspect a great deal more could and should be attempted in this respect). But perhaps here, as everywhere else, we must rest in the assurance that all our writing, all our reading, all our living, continues under the mercy of God.

Let us bless the Lord.
Thanks be to God.

Bibliography

The Alternative Service Book 1980, The Church of England (London: Collins, 1980).

Anselm, *Proslogion: Fides quaerens intellectum*, trans. M.J. Charlesworth (Oxford: Clarendon, 1965).

Aristotle, *Ethics: The Nicomachean Ethics*, trans. J.A.K. Thomson (Harmondsworth: Penguin, 1955).

Athanasius, *On the Incarnation*, trans. A Religious (London: Mowbray, 1953).

Attridge, Harold W., *A Commentary on the Epistle to the Hebrews*, ed. Helmut Koester (Philadelphia, PA: Fortress Press, 1989).

Augustine, Aurelius, *On Christian Doctrine*, trans. J.F. Shaw, in *A Select Library of the Nicene and Post-Nicene Fathers of the Christian Church*, First Series, vol. 2, ed. Philip Schaff (Grand Rapids and Edinburgh: Eerdmans and T & T Clark, 1993), pp. 513-97.

—, *On the Holy Trinity*, trans. A.W. Haddan, in *A Select Library of the Nicene and Post-Nicene Fathers of the Christian Church*, First Series, vol. 3, ed. Philip Schaff (Grand Rapids and Edinburgh: Eerdmans and T & T Clark, 1993), pp. 17-228.

—, *On Marriage and Concupiscence*, trans. Peter Holmes, Robert Ernest Wallis, revised Benjamin B. Warfield, in *A Select Library of the Nicene and Post-Nicene Fathers of the Christian Church*, First Series, vol. 5, ed. Philip Schaff (Grand Rapids and Edinburgh: Eerdmans and T & T Clark, 1991), pp. 263-308;

Aulén G., *Christus Victor: An Historical Study of the Three Main Types of the Idea of the Atonement*, trans. A.G. Herbert (London: SPCK, 1931).

Barth, Karl, *Church Dogmatics*, vols. I–IV, Eng. trans. and eds. G.W. Bromiley and T.F. Torrance (Edinburgh: T & T Clark, 1956–75).

—, *The Humanity of God*, trans. John Newton Thomas and Thomas Wieser, Fontana Library of Theology and Philosophy (London and Glasgow: Collins, 1961).

—, *Prayer and Preaching* (London: SCM Press, 1964).

The Book of Common Prayer, The Church of England (London: Oxford University Press, n.d.).

Celebrating Common Prayer: A Version of The Daily Office SSF, The European Province of the Society of Saint Francis (London: Mowbray, 1992).

Coakley, Sarah, '"Femininity" and the Holy Spirit', in Monica Furlong (ed.), *Mirror to the Church: Reflections on Sexism* (London: SPCK, 1988), pp. 124-35.

Colwell, John E., *Living the Christian Story: The Distinctiveness of Christian Ethics* (Edinburgh and New York: T & T Clark, 2001).

—, *Promise and Presence: An Exploration of Sacramental Theology* (Milton Keynes: Paternoster, 2005).

Daly, Mary, *Beyond God the Father: Towards a Philosophy of Women's Liberation* (London: Women's Press, 1986).

Derrida, Jacques, *Of Grammatology*, trans. Gayatri Chakravorty Spivak (Baltimore: John Hopkins Press, 1974).

deSilva, David A., *Perseverance in Gratitude: A Socio-Rhetorical Commentary on the Epistle "to the Hebrews"* (Grand Rapids, MI: Eerdmans, 2000).

Edwards, Jonathan, *The Works of Jonathan Edwards*, gen. ed. (vols. 1–2) Perry Miller, gen. ed. (vols. 3–9) John E. Smith, gen. ed. (vols. 10–23) Harry S. Stout (New Haven, CT: Yale University Press, 1957–).

Farrow, Douglas, 'St. Irenaeus of Lyons: The Church and the World', *Pro Ecclesia* 4.3 (1995), pp. 333-55.

—, *Ascension and Ecclesia: On the Significance of the Doctrine of the Ascension for Ecclesiology and Christian Cosmology* (Edinburgh: T & T Clark, 1999).

Fish, Stanley, *Is There a Text in This Class? The Authority of Interpretive Communities* (Cambridge, MA, and London: Harvard University Press, 1980).

Gorringe, T.J., *God's Just Vengeance: Crime, Violence and the Rhetoric of Salvation* (Cambridge: Cambridge University Press, 1996).

Grass, Tim, and Randall, Ian, 'C.H. Spurgeon on the Sacraments', in Anthony R. Cross and Philip E. Thompson (eds), *Baptist Sacramentalism* (Carlisle: Paternoster Press, 2003), 55-75.

Gregory Nazianzus, *Epistle to Cledonius the Priest Against Apollinarus*, in *A Select Library of the Nicene and Post-Nicene Fathers of the Christian Church*, Second Series, ed. Philip Schaff and Henry Wace, vol. 7 (Grand Rapids, MI: Eerdmans, 1989), pp. 439-43.

Gunton, Colin E., *Christ and Creation: The Didsbury Lectures 1990* (Carlisle and Grand Rapids, MI: Paternoster Press and Eerdmans, 1992).

—, *The One, The Three and the Many: God, Creation and the Culture of Modernity*, The Bampton Lectures 1992 (Cambridge: Cambridge University Press, 1993).

—, *A Brief Theology of Revelation* (Edinburgh: T & T Clark, 1995).

—, *The Triune Creator: A Historical and Systematic Study* (Edinburgh: Edinburgh University Press, 1998).

Hampson, Daphne, *Theology and Feminism* (Oxford: Blackwell, 1990).

Hartshorne, Charles, *Man's Vision of God and the Logic of Theism* (New York: Harper, 1941).

Hauerwas, Stanley, *Character and the Christian Life: A Study in Theological Ethics* (Notre Dame, IN, and London: University of Notre Dame Press, 1994; originally published San Antonio, TX: Trinity University Press, 1975).

—, *The Peacable Kingdom: A Primer in Christian Ethics* (London: SCM Press, 1984).

—, *Christian Existence Today: Essays on Church, World, and Living In Between* (Durham, NC: Labyrinth, 1988).

—, *In Good Company: The Church as Polis* (Notre Dame, IN, and London: University of Notre Dame Press, 1995).

—, *Sanctify Them in the Truth: Holiness Exemplified* (Edinburgh: T & T Clark, 1998).

Hector, Kevin W., 'God's Triunity and Self-Determination: A Conversation with Karl Barth, Bruce McCormack and Paul Molnar', *International Journal of Systematic Theology* 7.3 (2005), pp. 246-61.

Hemming, Laurence Paul, '*Analogia non Entis sed Entitatis*: The Ontological Consequences of the Doctrine of Analogy', *International Journal of Systematic Theology* 6.2 (2004), pp. 118-29.

Holmes, Stephen R., *Listening to the Past: The Place of Tradition in Theology* (Carlisle: Paternoster Press, 2002).

Irenaeus, *Against Heresies*, in *The Ante-Nicene Fathers*, vol. 1, ed. Alexander Roberts, James Donaldson and A. Cleveland Coxe (Grand Rapids, MI: Eerdmans, 1987), pp. 315-567.

Irving, Edward, *Christ's Holiness in Flesh, The Form, Fountain Head, and Assurance to us of Holiness in Flesh* (Edinburgh: John Lindsay, 1831).

Jenson, Robert W., *God after God: The God of the Past and the Future as Seen in the Work of Karl Barth* (Indianapolis and New York: Bobbs-Merrill, 1969).

—, 'What is the Point of Trinitarian Theology?', in Christoph Schwöbel (ed.), *Trinitarian Theology Today: Essays on Divine Being and Act* (Edinburgh: T & T Clark, 1995), pp. 31–43.

—, *Systematic Theology*, vol. 2, *The Works of God* (Oxford and New York: Oxford University Press, 1999).

Jüngel, Eberhard, '*…keine Menschenlosigkeit Gottes…*Zur Theologie Karl Barths zwischen Theismus und Atheismus', *Evangelische Theologie*, 31 (1971), pp. 376-90.

—, *The Doctrine of the Trinity: God's Being is in Becoming*, trans. Horton Harris (Edinburgh: Scottish Academic Press, 1976).

Lincoln, Andrew T., *Hebrews: A Guide* (London: T & T Clark, 2006).

Lindars, Barnabas, *The Theology of the Letter to the Hebrews* (Cambridge: Cambridge University Press, 1991).

MacFague, Sally, *The Body of God: An Ecological Theology* (London: SCM Press, 1993).

MacGregor, Neil, and Langmuir, Erika, *Seeing Salvation: Images of Christ in Art* (New Haven, CT: Yale, 2000).

McCormack, Bruce L., 'Karl Barth's Christology as a Resource for a Reformed Version of Kenoticism', *International Journal of Systematic Theology* 8.3 (2006), pp. 243-51.

McGonigle, Herbert, *Sufficient Saving Grace: John Wesley's Evangelical Arminianism* (Carlisle: Paternoster Press, 2001).

Molnar, Paul D., 'The Trinity, Election and God's Ontological Freedom: A Response to Kevin W. Hector', *International Journal of Systematic Theology* 8.3 (2006), pp. 294-306.

Moltmann, Jürgen, *The Trinity and the Kingdom of God: The Doctrine of God*, trans. Margaret Kohl (London: SCM Press, 1981).

Nietzsche, Friedrich, *Thus Spoke Zarathustra*, trans. R.J. Hollingdale (Harmondsworth: Penguin, 1971).

O'Donovan, Oliver, *The Desire of the Nations: Rediscovering the Roots of Political Theology* (Cambridge: Cambridge University Press, 1996).

Owen, John, *A Discourse concerning the Holy Spirit* (1674), in *The Works of John Owen*, vol. 3, ed. W.H. Goold (London: Banner of Truth, 1965).

—, *The Death of Death in the Death of Christ*, in *The Works of John Owen*, vol. 10, ed. W.H. Goold (London: Banner of Truth, 1967), pp. 140-421.

Pannenberg, Wolfhart, *Systematic Theology*, vol. 1, trans. Geoffrey Bromiley (Grand Rapids, MI: Eerdmans, 1991).

Rogers, Eugene F., Jr., *After the Spirit: A Constructive Pneumatology from Resources Outside the Modern West* (London: SCM Press, 2006).

Ruether, Rosemary Radford, 'The Female Nature of God: A Problem in Contemporary Religious Life', in J.B. Metz and E. Schillebeeckx (eds), *'God as Father?': Concilium* 143 (New York and Edinburgh: Seabury Press and T & T Clark, 1981), pp. 61-66.

Tanner, Kathryn, *Jesus, Humanity and the Trinity: A Brief Systematic Theology* (Edinburgh: T & T Clark, 2001).

Thomas Aquinas, *Summa Theologica*, trans. by Fathers of the English Dominican Province (Westminster, MD: Christian Classics, 1981).

Wadell, Paul J., *The Primacy of Love: An Introduction to the Ethics of Thomas Aquinas* (New York and Mahwah: Paulist Press, 1992).

Wesley, John, *A Plain Account of Christian Perfection as believed and taught by the Reverend Mr. John Wesley, from the year 1725, to the year 1777*, in *The Works of the Rev. John Wesley*, vol. 11 (London: Wesleyan Conference Office, 1872), pp. 366-446.

Young, Frances, '"Creatio ex Nihilo": A Context for the Emergence of the Christian Doctrine of Creation', *Scottish Journal of Theology* 44 (1991), pp. 139-51.

Scripture Index

Name Index

Subject Index